Contents

Welcome to
Kindergarten

Name _____

A B C D E F G H I J K L M N O P Q R S T U V W X Y Z

A

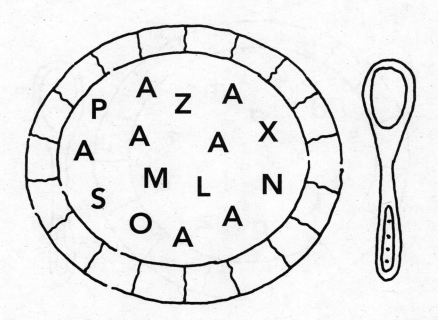

Children

- write *A* in the box
- circle all the *A*'s in the bowl of alphabet soup

 HOME CONNECTION

I am learning about big *A*.
Let me show you all the big *A*'s
in the alphabet soup.

Welcome to
Kindergarten

Name _____

a b c d e f g h i j k l m n o p q r s t u v w x y z

a

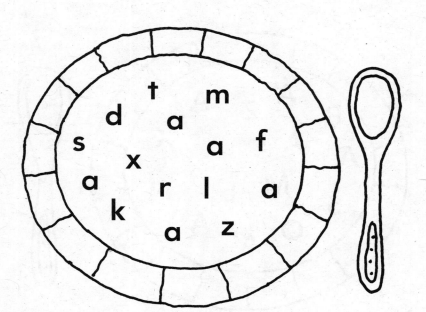

Children
- write *a* in the box
- circle all the *a*'s in the bowl of alphabet soup

 HOME CONNECTION

I am learning about small *a*.
Let me show you all the small *a*'s
in the alphabet soup.

2

Welcome to
Kindergarten

Name _____

Children

• write their names
• draw pictures of themselves

HOME CONNECTION

I am learning to write my name.
Help me write it at home, too.

3

Welcome to Kindergarten

Name _____

A B C D E F G H I J K L M N O P Q R S T U V W X Y Z

B

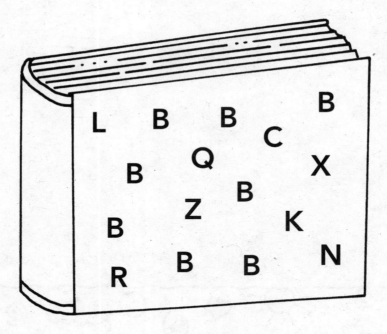

Children

• write *B* in the box
• circle all the *B*'s in the book

HOME CONNECTION

I am learning about big *B*.
Let me show you all the big *B*'s
in the book.

4

Welcome to
Kindergarten

Name _____

a b c d e f g h i j k l m n o p q r s t u v w x y z

b

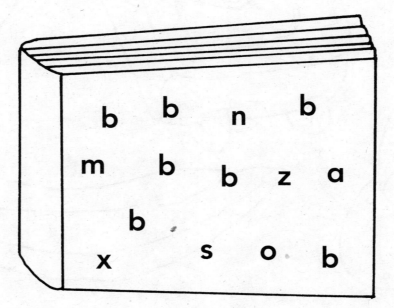

Children

- write *b* in the box
- circle all the *b*'s in the book

HOME CONNECTION

I am learning about small *b*.
Let me show you all the small *b*'s
in the book.

Welcome to
Kindergarten

Name _____

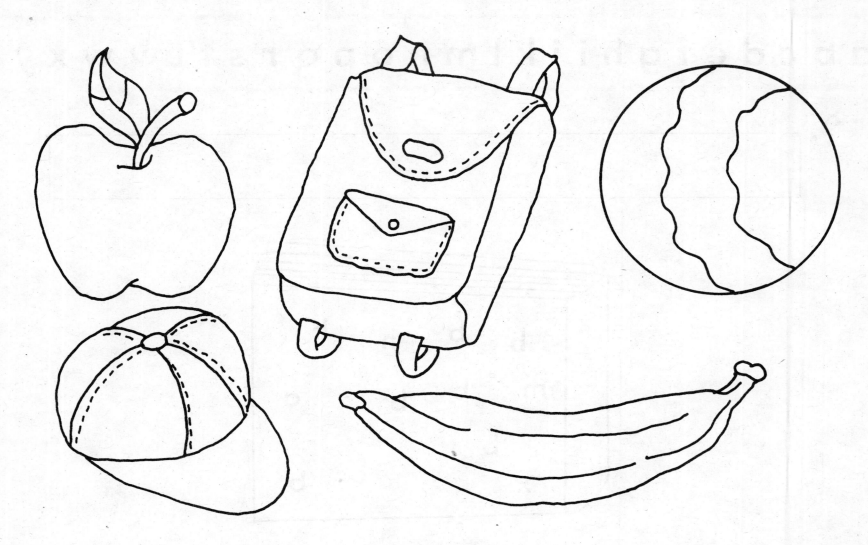

Children

- color the apple red, the banana yellow, the cap blue, the ball green, and the backpack orange
- say the names of the colors

 HOME CONNECTION

I am learning colors. Ask me to name the colors I know so far. Help me learn some new ones!

6

Welcome to
Kindergarten

Name _____

A B C D E F G H I J K L M N O P Q R S T U V W X Y Z

C

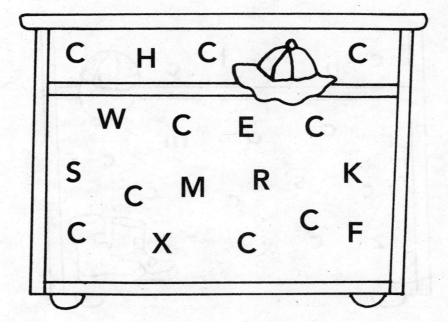

C H C C
W C E C
S C M R K
C X C C F

Children

- write *C* in the box
- circle all the *C*'s in the cubby

HOME CONNECTION

I am learning about big *C*.
Let me show you all the big *C*'s
in the cubby.

Welcome to
Kindergarten

Name _____

a b c d e f g h i j k l m n o p q r s t u v w x y z

C

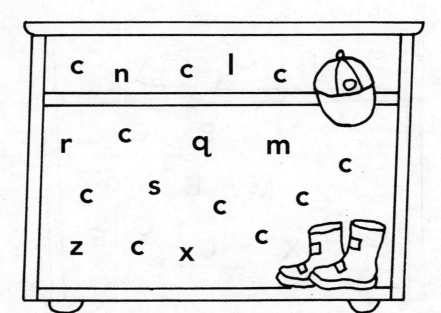

Children

- write *c* in the box
- circle all the *c*'s in the cubby

HOME CONNECTION

I am learning about small *c*.
Let me show you all the small *c*'s
in the cubby.

8

Welcome to
Kindergarten

Name _____

1.

2.

3.

Children

• circle two things that go together in each row
• name the pair

 HOME CONNECTION

I am learning about things that go together. Help me find pairs of things at home.

Welcome to Kindergarten

Name _____

ABCDEFGHIJKLMNOPQRSTUVWXYZ

D

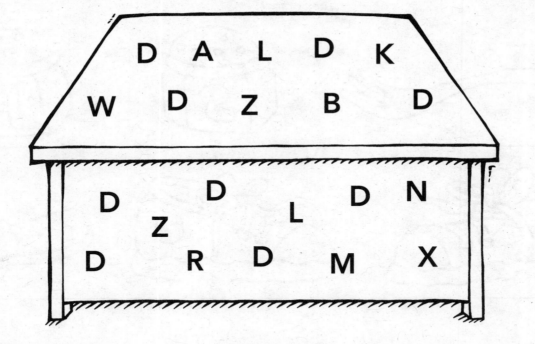

Children
- write *D* in the box
- circle all the *D*'s on the desk

HOME CONNECTION

I am learning about big *D*.
Let me show you all the big *D*'s
on the desk.

10

Welcome to Kindergarten

Name _____

a b c d e f g h i j k l m n o p q r s t u v w x y z

d

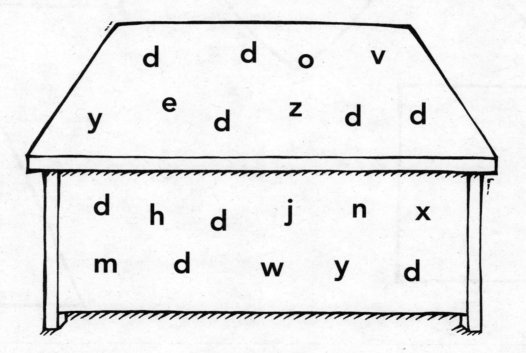

Children
- write _d_ in the box
- circle all the _d_'s on the desk

HOME CONNECTION

I am learning about small _d_. Let me show you all the small _d_'s on the desk.

Welcome to Kindergarten

Name _____

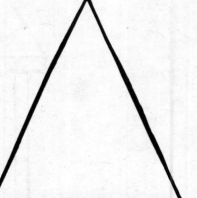

Children

- find the circle and color it red
- find the triangle and color it blue
- find the rectangle and color it yellow
- find the square and color it brown

 HOME CONNECTION

I am learning about shapes. Help me find these shapes in things at home.

Welcome to **Kindergarten**

Name _____

ABCDEFGHIJKLMNOPQRSTUVWXYZ

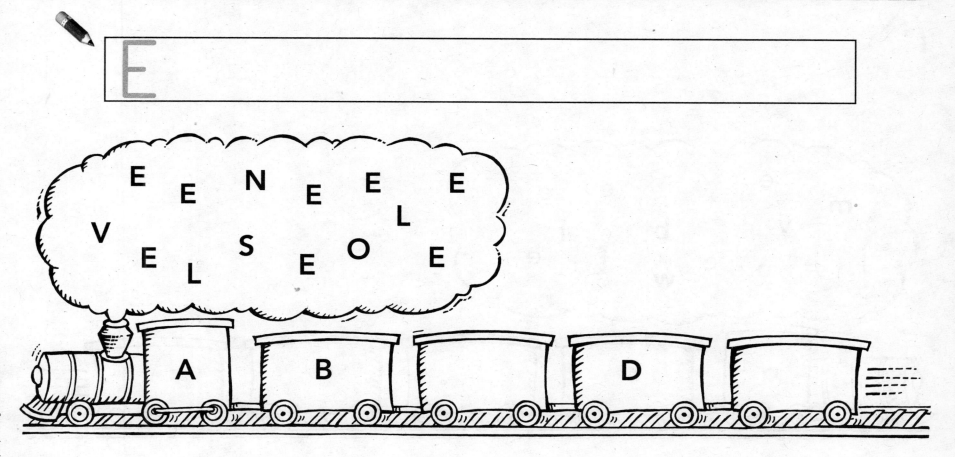

E

Children

- write *E* in the box
- circle all the *E*'s in the steam from the engine
- write the missing capital letters on the alphabet train

HOME CONNECTION

I am learning about big *E*.
Let me show you all the big *E*'s
in the picture. Then let's read
the letters on the alphabet train.

13

Welcome to Kindergarten

Name _____

a b c d e f g h i j k l m n o p q r s t u v w x y z

e = 9 H I I K L M N O P Q R S T U W X

m e r k e e
j e v b l
j e p e f e
w

a   b   c   d   e

Children
- write _e_ in the box
- circle all the _e_'s in the steam from the engine
- write the missing lowercase letters on the alphabet train

14

 HOME CONNECTION

I am learning about small _e_. Let me show you all the small _e_'s in the picture. Then let's read the letters on the alphabet train.

Welcome to Kindergarten

Name _____

a b c d e f g h i j k l m n o p q r s t u v w x y z

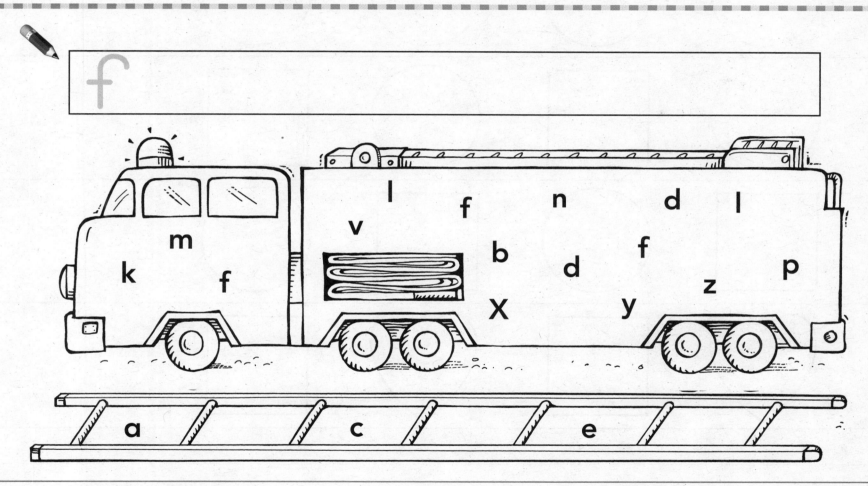

Children

- write *f* in the box
- circle all the *f*'s on the fire engine
- write the missing lowercase letters on the alphabet ladder

HOME CONNECTION

I am learning about small *f*. Let me show you all the small *f*'s on the fire engine. Then let's read the letters on the alphabet ladder.

Welcome to
Kindergarten

Name _____

1. ◯ ◯ ◯ ◯

2. ◯ ▢ ◯ ▢

3. ▢ ◯ ▢ ◯

4. ♡ ▢ ♡ ▢

Children
- name the pictures in each row
- draw what comes next in the pattern

 HOME CONNECTION

I am learning about patterns. Can we find some patterns at home? (Hint: Clothing or wallpaper with stripes is a good place to start!)

18

Welcome to
Kindergarten

Name _____

ABCDEFGHIJKLMNOPQRSTUVWXYZ

G

Children

- write _G_ in the box
- circle all the _G_'s on the garage
- write the missing capital letters on the alphabet cars

HOME CONNECTION

I am learning about big _G_.
Let me show you all the big _G_'s
on the garage. Then let's read
the letters on the alphabet cars.

19

Welcome to **Kindergarten**

Name _____

a b c d e f g h i j k l m n o p q r s t u v w x y z

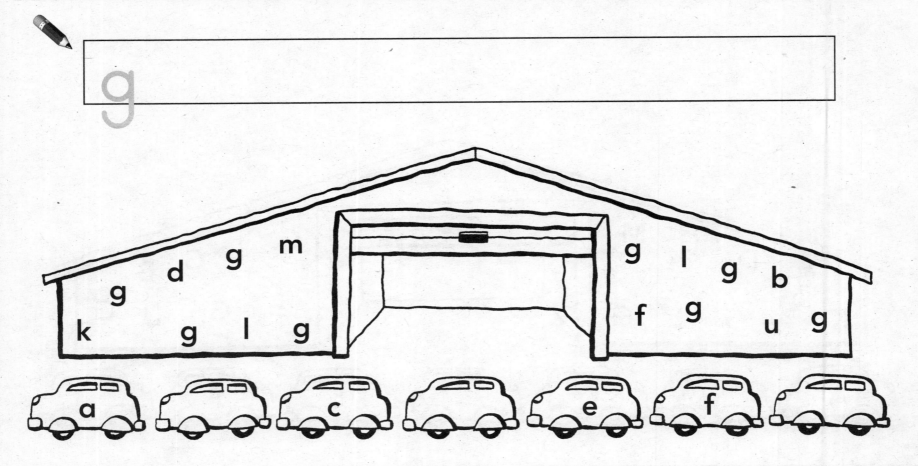

g

Children

- write *g* in the box
- circle all the *g*'s on the garage
- write the missing lowercase letters on the alphabet cars

HOME CONNECTION

I am learning about small *g*.
Let me show you all the small *g*'s
on the garage. Then let's read
the letters on the alphabet cars.

20

Welcome to
Kindergarten

Name _____

1	2	3

Children
- say each number
- draw balloons to show the number

 HOME CONNECTION

I am learning to count. Help me count things as I set the table.

Welcome to Kindergarten

Name _____

A B C D E F G H I J K L M N O P Q R S T U V W X Y Z

H

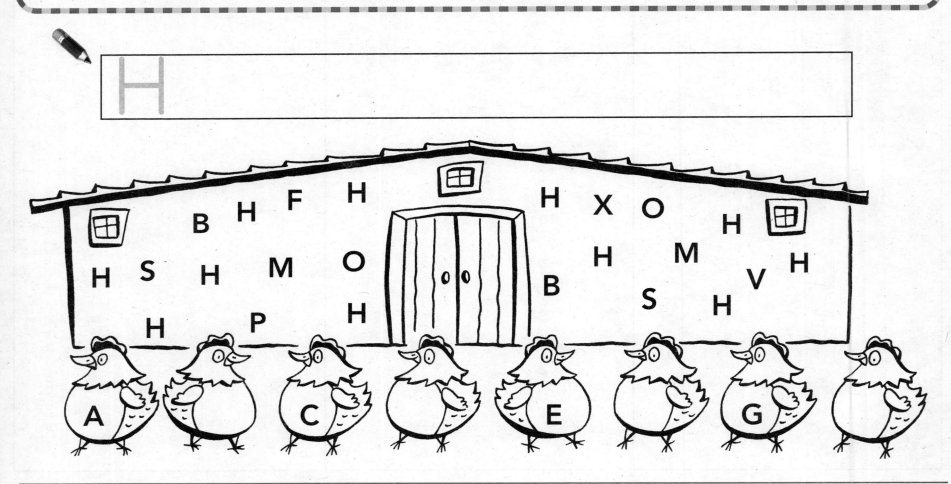

Children

- write *H* in the box
- circle all the *H*'s on the henhouse
- write the missing capital letters on the alphabet hens

 HOME CONNECTION

I am learning about big *H*. Let me show you all the big *H*'s on the henhouse. Then let's read the letters on the alphabet hens.

Welcome to
Kindergarten

Name _____

a b c d e f g h i j k l m n o p q r s t u v w x y z

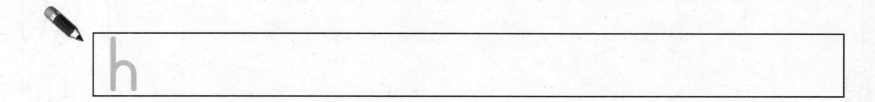

h

Children

- write *h* in the box
- circle all the *h*'s on the henhouse
- write the missing lowercase letters on the alphabet hens

HOME CONNECTION

I am learning about small *h*.
Let me show you all the small *h*'s
on the henhouse. Then let's read
the letters on the alphabet hens.

23

Welcome to **Kindergarten**

Name _____

Children

- write the numbers 1 to 10
- write more numbers if they can

 HOME CONNECTION

I am learning to write numbers.
Help me write them at home, too.

Welcome to
Kindergarten

Name _____

ABCDEFGHIJKLMNOPQRSTUVWXYZ

Children

- write *I* in the box
- circle all the *I*'s on the igloo
- write the missing capital letters on the alphabet penguins

HOME CONNECTION

I am learning about big *I*.
Let me show you all the big *I*'s
on the igloo. Then let's read the
letters on the alphabet penguins.

25

Welcome to Kindergarten

Name _____

a b c d e f g h i j k l m n o p q r s t u v w x y z

i

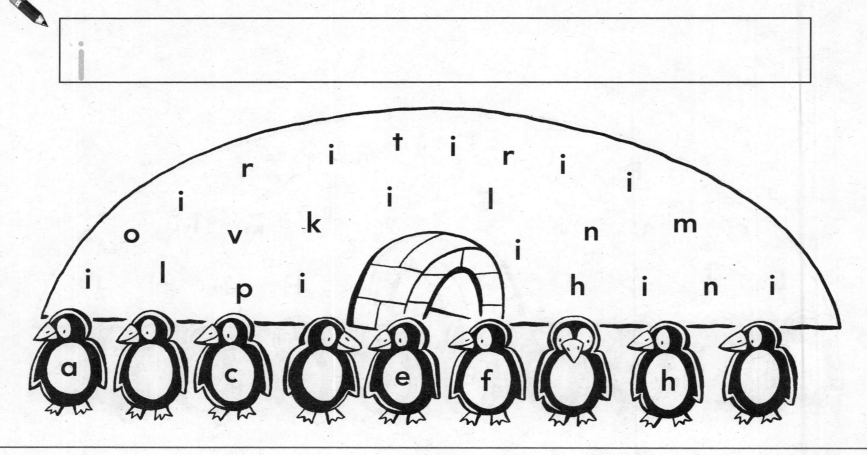

Children

- write *i* in the box
- circle all the *i*'s on the igloo
- write the missing lowercase letters on the alphabet penguins

HOME CONNECTION

I am learning about small *i*. Let me show you all the small *i*'s on the igloo. Then let's read the letters on the alphabet penguins.

26

Welcome to
Kindergarten

Name _____

STOP

Children
- tell what they see in each picture
- say what the sign tells them to do

 HOME CONNECTION

I am learning about signs. Let's look for these signs when we go out together.

27

Welcome to Kindergarten

Name _____

ABCDEFGHIJKLMNOPQRSTUVWXYZ

J

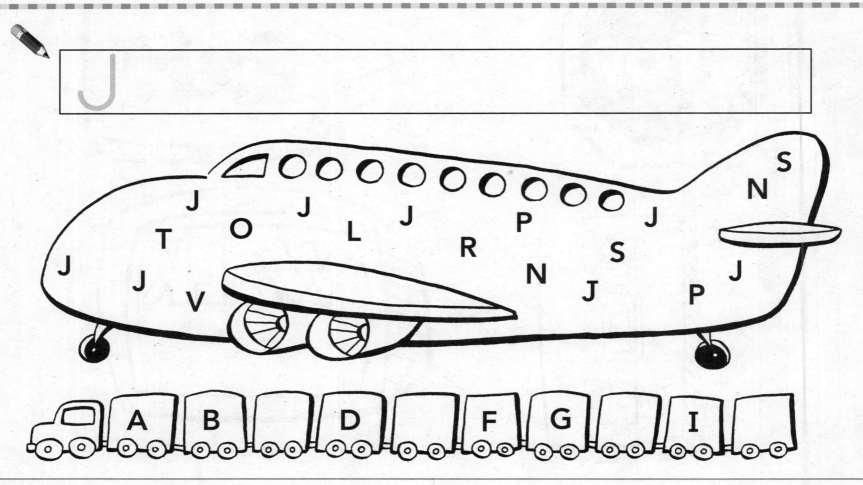

Children

- write *J* in the box
- circle all the *J*'s on the jet
- write the missing capital letters on the alphabet carts

28

HOME CONNECTION

I am learning about big *J*. Let me show you all the big *J*'s on the jet. Then let's read the letters on the alphabet carts.

Welcome to Kindergarten

Name _____

a b c d e f g h i j k l m n o p q r s t u v w x y z

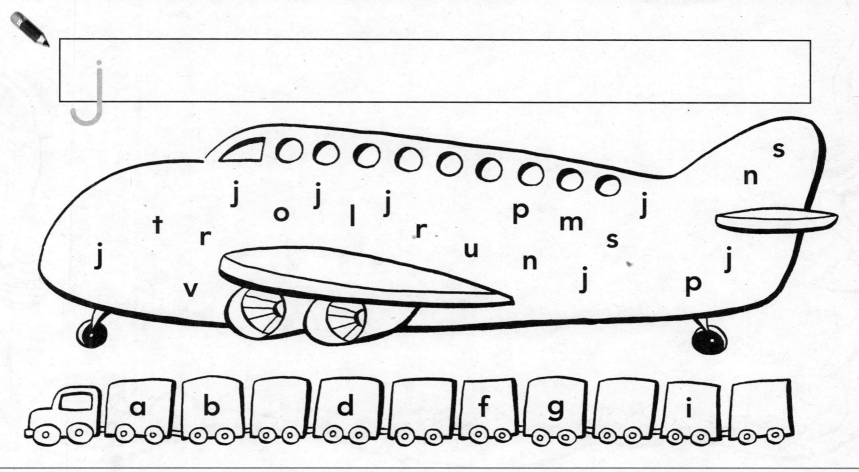

j

Children

- write *j* in the box
- circle all the *j*'s on the jet
- write the missing lowercase letters on the alphabet carts

HOME CONNECTION

I am learning about small *j*. Let me show you all the small *j*'s on the jet. Then let's read the letters on the alphabet carts.

29

Welcome to
Kindergarten

Name _____

 Children

- write all the words they know how to write
- read each word they've written

 HOME CONNECTION

I can write some words. Let me read them to you.

Name _____

THEME 1: Look at Us!
Week One *Now I'm Big*
Compare and Contrast, Responding

Children
• look at the pictures of things babies eat, wear, ride, and play with
• draw pictures of things they eat, wear, ride, and play with

 Home Connection
Let me tell you about a book called *Now I'm Big*. Then I can tell you how my pictures show I've grown.

Name _____

ABCDEFGHIJKLMNOPQRSTUVWXYZ

K

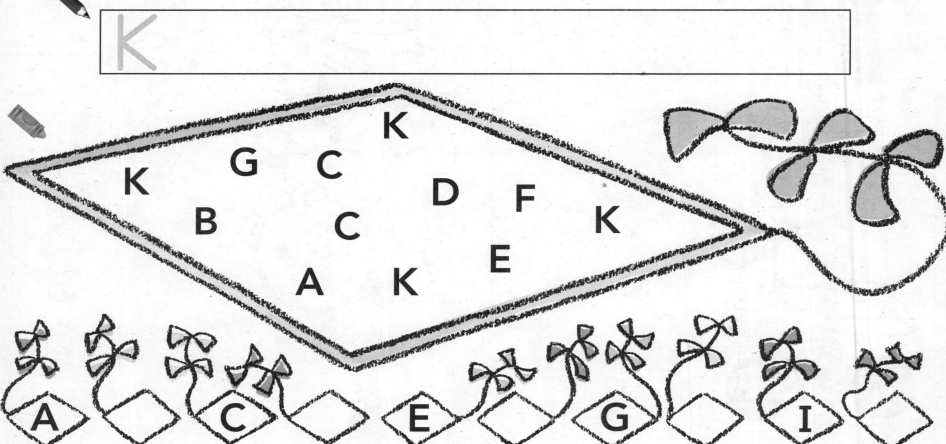

K G C K
B C D F K
A C E
A K

A C E G I

THEME 1: Look at Us!
Week One
Letter Name *Kk*

Children
- write *K* in the box
- circle all the *K*'s on the kite
- write the missing capital letters on the small kites

 Home Connection
I am learning about big *K*. Let me show you all the big *K*'s on the kite. Then let's read the letters on the alphabet kites.

32

Name _____

a b c d e f g h i j k l m n o p q r s t u v w x y z

k

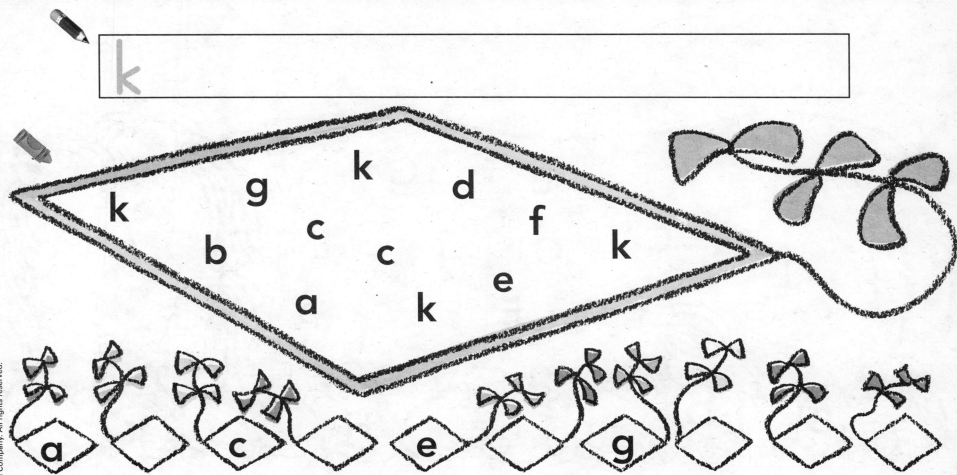

k

g   k

b   c   d

k   c   c   f

a   e   k

k

a   c   e   g

THEME 1: Look at Us!
Week One
Letter Name Kk

Children
- write *k* in the box
- circle all the *k*'s on the kite
- write the missing lowercase letters on the small kites

 Home Connection
I am learning about small *k*.
Let me show you all the small *k*'s
on the kite. Then let's read the
letters on the alphabet kites.

33

Name _____

ABCDEFGHIJKLMNOPQRSTUVWXYZ

L

THEME 1: Look at Us!
Week One
Letter Name *Ll*

34

Children
• write *L* in the box
• circle all the *L*'s on the lion
• write the missing capital letters on the small lions

Home Connection
I am learning about big *L*. Let me show you all the big *L*'s on the lion. Then let's read the letters on the small lions.

Name _____

a b c d e f g h i j k l m n o p q r s t u v w x y z

THEME 1: Look at Us!
Week One
Letter Name *Ll*

Children
- write *l* in the box
- circle all the *l*'s on the lion
- write the missing lowercase letters on the small lions

 Home Connection
I am learning about small *l*.
Let me show you all the small *l*'s on the lion. Then let's read the letters on the small lions.

35

Name _____

THEME 1: Look at Us!
Week One *Mice Squeak, We Speak*
Compare and Contrast, Responding

Children
- circle an animal that squeaks
- color green an animal that croaks
- circle an animal that moos
- color yellow an animal that quacks
- underline those who can speak

 Home Connection
Let me tell you a story called
Mice Squeak, We Speak. Then I
can tell you what my picture
shows.

36

Name _____

ABCDEFGHIJKLMNOPQRSTUVWXYZ

M

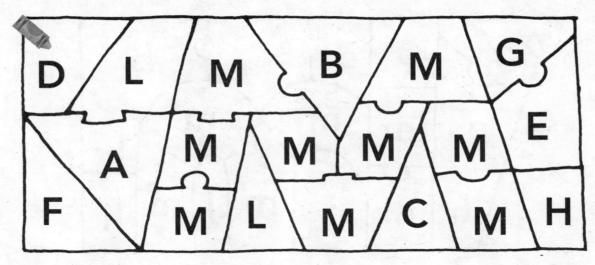

 k

 m

 h

THEME 1: Look at Us!
Week One
Letter Name Mm

Children
- color every puzzle piece with *M* red
- see what shapes the red pieces make
- write the matching capital letter on the mice

Home Connection
I am learning about big *M*.
Let me show you all the big *M*'s
on the puzzle. Then let's read
the matching letters on the mice.

37

Name _____

abcdefghijklmnopqrstuvwxyz

m

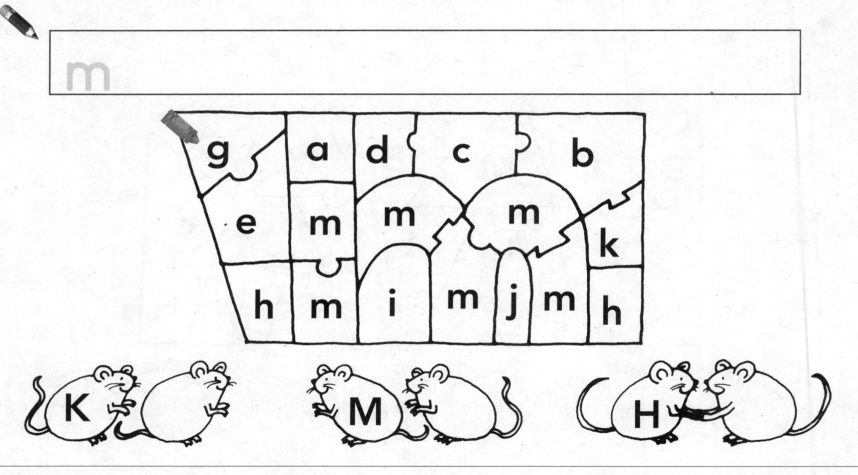

THEME 1: Look at Us!
Week One
Letter Name Mm

Children
- color every puzzle piece with *m* blue
- see what shapes the blue pieces make
- write the matching lowercase letter on the mice

 Home Connection
I am learning about small *m*.
Let me show you all the small *m*'s
on the puzzle. Then let's read the
matching letters on the mice.

38

Name _____

N _____

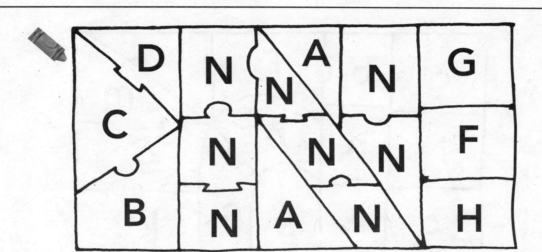

THEME 1: Look at Us!
Week One
Letter Name Nn

Children
- color every puzzle piece with *N* green
- see what shape the green pieces make
- write the matching capital letter on the birds

 Home Connection
I am learning about big *N*.
Let me show you all the big *N*'s
on the puzzle. Then let's read
the matching letters on the birds.

Name _____

a b c d e f g h i j k l m n o p q r s t u v w x y z

n

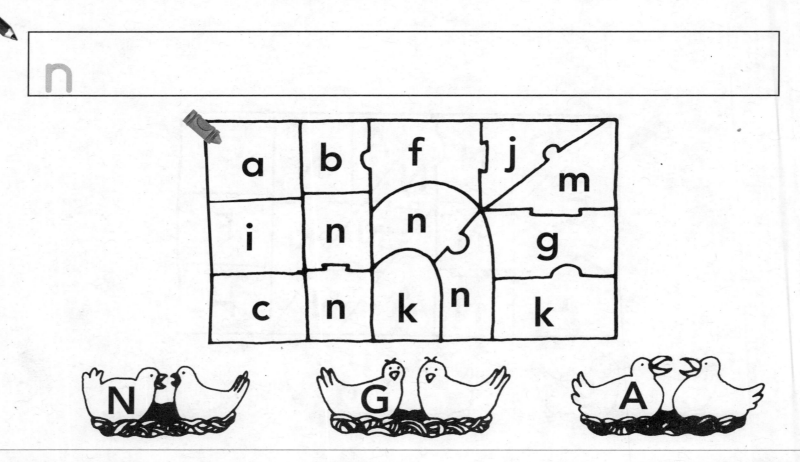

THEME 1: Look at Us!
Week One
Letter Name Nn

Children
• color every puzzle piece with *n* yellow
• see what shape the yellow pieces make
• write the matching lowercase letter on the birds

 Home Connection
I am learning about small *n*.
Let me show you all the small *n*'s
on the puzzle. Then let's read the
matching letters on the birds.

Name _____

ABCDEFGHIJKLMNOPQRSTUVWXYZ

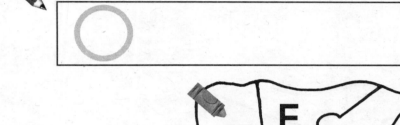

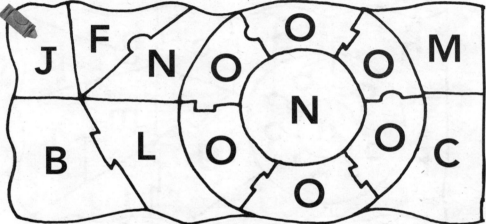

THEME 1: Look at Us!
Week One
Letter Name *Oo*

Children
- color every puzzle piece with *O* purple
- see what shape the purple pieces make
- write the matching capital letter on the octopuses

Home Connection
I am learning about big *O*. Let me show you all the big *O*'s on the puzzle. Then let's read the matching letters on the octopuses.

41

Name _____

abcdefghijklmnopqrstuvwxyz

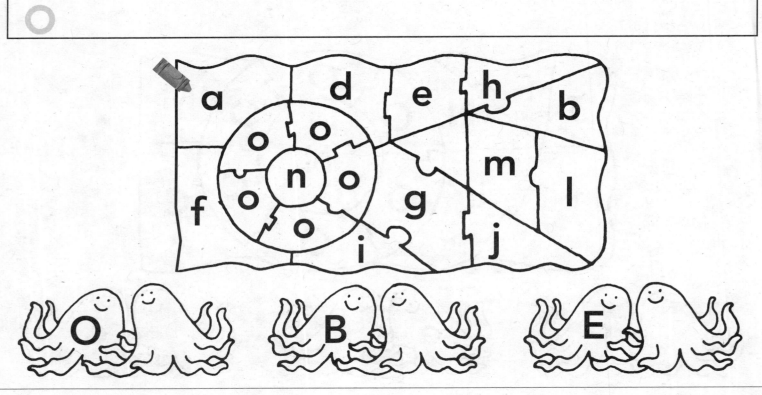

THEME 1: Look at Us!
Week One
Letter Name *Oo*

Children
- color every puzzle piece with *o* orange
- see what shape the orange pieces make
- write the matching lowercase letter on the octopuses

Home Connection
I am learning about small *o*.
Let me show you all the small *o*'s on the puzzle. Then let's read the matching letters on the octopuses.

Just for fun, color the gingerbread people! What colors did you choose?

43

Name _____

1.

2.

THEME 1: Look At Us!
Week Two *The Gingerbread Man*
Noting Important Details

44

Children
- color the cookie that looks like the Gingerbread Man in the story
- color the characters who chased after the Gingerbread Man

Home Connection
Let me tell you the story *The Gingerbread Man.*

Name _____

THEME 1: Look at Us!
Week Two _The Gingerbread Man_
Responding

Children
- decorate their own gingerbread man

 Home Connection
Today I decorated this gingerbread man. Maybe some weekend we could make gingerbread cookies together!

45

Name _____

ABCDEFGHIJKLMNOPQRSTUVWXYZ

P

 c

 p

 m

THEME 1: Look at Us!
Week Two
Letter Name *Pp*

Children
- write *P* in the box
- circle all the *P*'s on the path
- color the circles to show Porcupine the path to the pizza
- write the matching capital letter on the small porcupines

 Home Connection
I am learning about big *P*. Let me show you all the big *P*'s on the path. Then let's read the matching letters on the small porcupines.

46

Name _____

a b c d e f g h i j k l m n o p q r s t u v w x y z

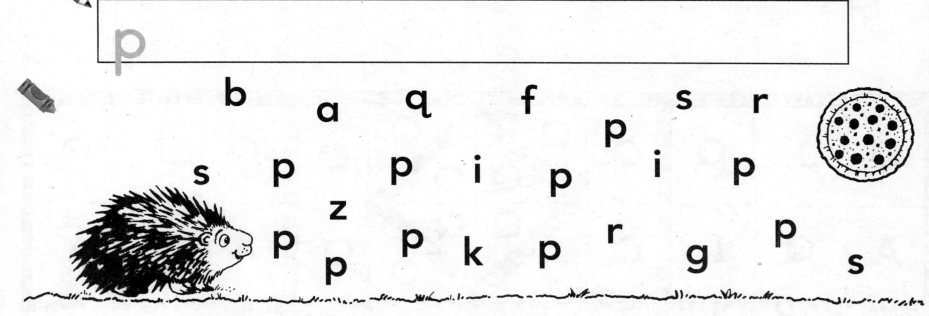

p

b   a   q   f   s   r

s   p   p   i   p   i   p

z

p   p   k   p   r   g   p

p   s

THEME 1: Look at Us!
Week Two
Letter Name *Pp*

Children
- write *p* in the box
- circle all the *p*'s on the path
- color the circles to show Porcupine the path to the pizza
- write the matching lowercase letter on the small porcupines

Home Connection
I am learning about small *p*. Let me show you all the small *p*'s on the path. Then let's read the matching letters on the small porcupines.

47

Name _____

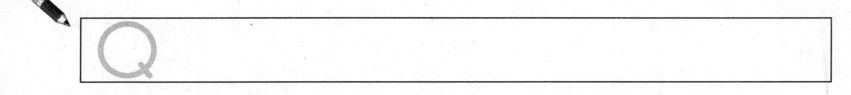
Q

 a

 j

 i

 q

THEME 1: Look at Us!
Week Two
Letter Name *Qq*

Children
- write *Q* in the box
- color all the *Q*'s red
- write the matching capital letter on the quilt squares

 Home Connection
I am learning about big *Q*. Let me show you all the big *Q*'s on the quilt. Then let's read the matching letters on the quilt squares.

48

Name _____

q

A

J

I

Q

THEME 1: Look at Us!
Week Two
Letter Name *Qq*

Children
- write *q* in the box
- color all the *q*'s blue
- write the matching lowercase letter on the quilt squares

Home Connection
I am learning about small *q*. Let me show you all the small *q*'s on the quilt. Then let's read the matching letters on the quilt squares.

49

Name _____

THEME 1: Look at Us!
Week Two *Here Are My Hands*
Noting Important Details

50

Children
- circle the body parts named in the book
- draw a picture of themselves, adding as much detail as they can

 Home Connection
Let me tell you about the book *Here Are My Hands*. Then I can tell you about this picture I drew of myself.

Name _____

A B C D E F G H I J K L M N O P Q R S T U V W X Y Z

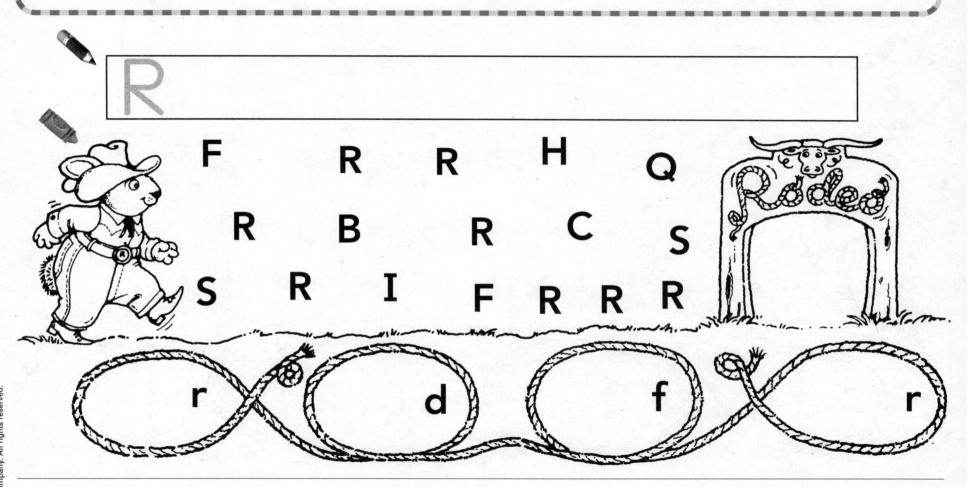

R

F	R	R		H		Q
R	B		R	C		S
S	R	I	F	R	R	R

r   d   f   r

THEME 1: Look at Us!
Week Two
Letter Name *Rr*

Children
• write *R* in the box
• circle all the *R*'s on the path
• color the circles to show Rabbit the path to the rodeo
• write the matching capital letter in the ropes

 Home Connection
I am learning about big *R*. Let me show you all the big *R*'s on the path. Then let's read the matching letters in the ropes.

Name _____

a b c d e f g h i j k l m n o p q r s t u v w x y z

r

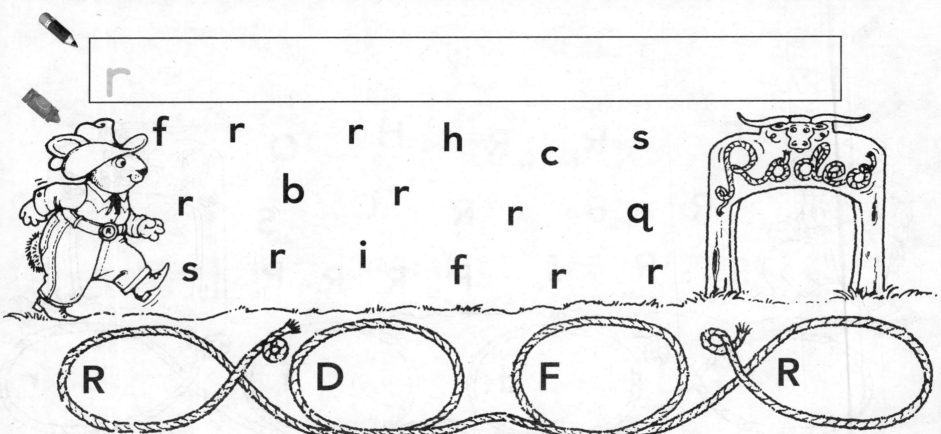

f r r h c s

r b r r q

r i r

s r i f r r

R D F R

THEME 1: Look at Us!
Week Two
Letter Name Rr

Children
- write *r* in the box
- circle all the *r*'s on the path
- color the circles to show Rabbit the path to the rodeo
- write the matching lowercase letter in the ropes

 Home Connection
I am learning about small *r*. Let me show you all the small *r*'s on the path. Then let's read the matching letters in the ropes.

Name _____

S

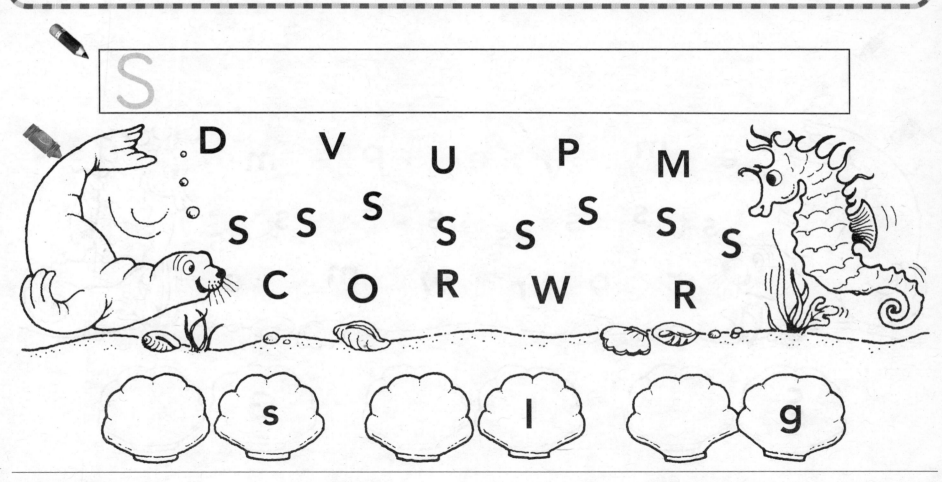

D	V	U	P	M
S	S	S	S	S
C	O	R	W	R

s   l   g

THEME 1: Look at Us!
Week Two
Letter Name _Ss_

Children
- write _S_ in the box
- circle all the _S_'s on the path
- color the circles to show Seal the path to the seahorse
- write the matching capital letter on the shells

Home Connection
I am learning about big _S_. Let me show you all the big _S_'s on the path. Then let's read the matching letters on the shells.

53

Name _____

a b c d e f g h i j k l m n o p q r s t u v w x y z

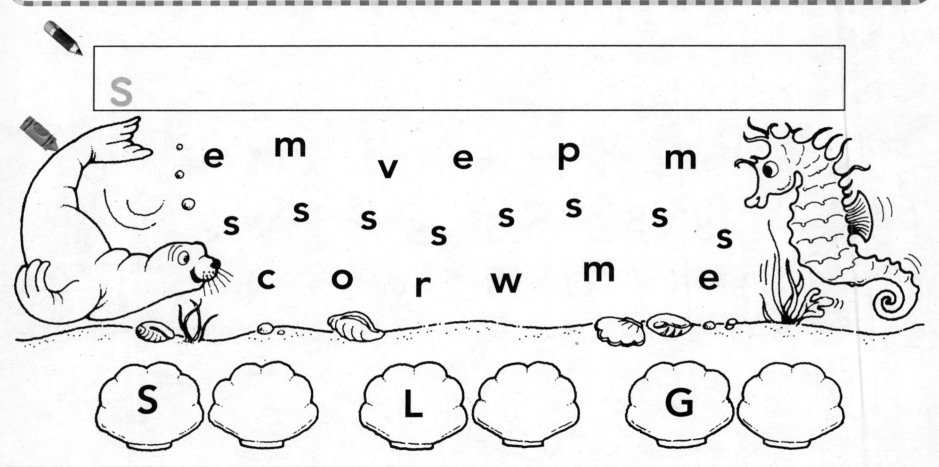

S

e m v e p m

s s s s s s

c o r w m e

S   L   G

THEME 1: Look at Us!
Week Two
Letter Name _Ss_

54

Children
- write _s_ in the box
- circle all the _s_'s on the path
- color the circles to show Seal the path to the seahorse
- write the matching lowercase letter on the shells

 Home Connection
I am learning about small _s_. Let me show you all the small _s_'s on the path. Then let's read the matching letters on the shells.

Name _____

ABCDEFGHIJKLMNOPQRSTUVWXYZ

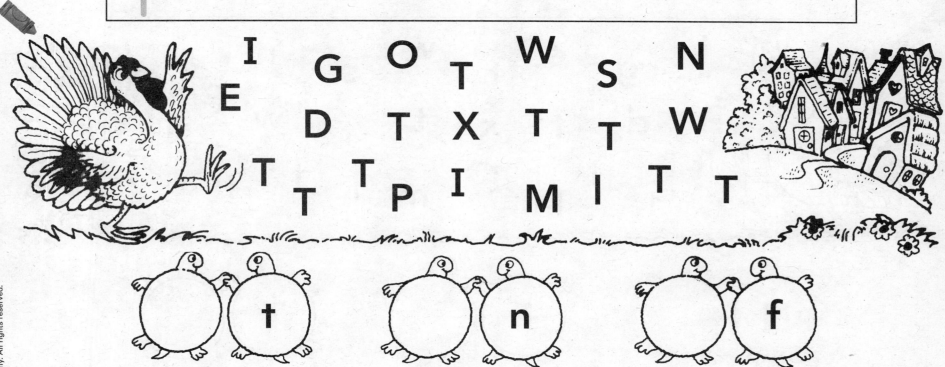

T

I G O T W S N
E D T X T T W
T T P I M I T T

t   n   f

THEME 1: Look at Us!
Week Two
Letter Name *Tt*

Children
• write *T* in the box
• circle all the *T*'s on the path
• color the circles to show Turkey the path to the town
• write the matching capital letter on the turtles

Home Connection
I am learning about big *T*. Let me show you all the big *T*'s on the path. Then let's read the matching letters on the turtles.

55

Name _____

a b c d e f g h i j k l m n o p q r s t u v w x y z

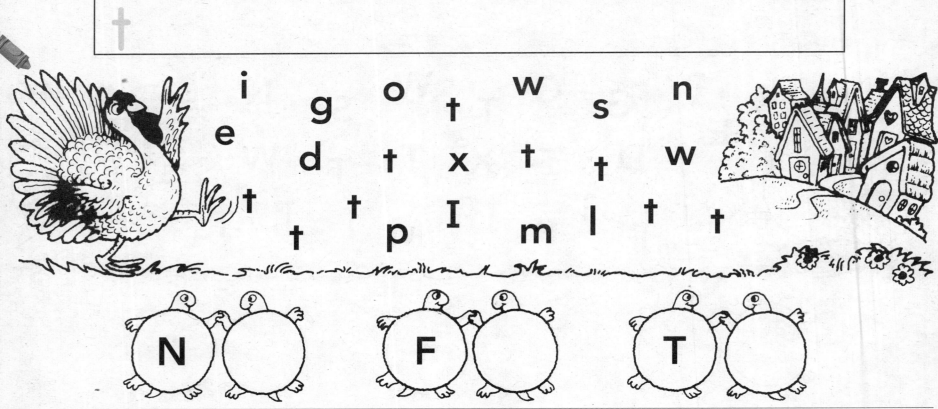

t

i g o w s n
e d t x t t w
t t p I m l t t

N F T

THEME 1: Look at Us!
Week Two
Letter Name *Tt*

Children
- write *t* in the box
- circle all the *t*'s on the path
- color the circles to show Turkey the path to the town
- write the matching lowercase letter on the turtles

Home Connection
I am learning about small *t*. Let me show you all the small *t*'s on the path. Then let's read the matching letters on the turtles.

56

Name _____

Theme 1: Look at Us!
Week Three *The City Mouse and
the Country Mouse*
Compare and Contrast

Children

• think about the differences between the city
and country scenes

• color the scene that is more like where they
live

 Home Connection
Let me tell you about *The City
Mouse and the Country Mouse* and
why I colored this picture.

57

Name _____

ABCDEFGHIJKLMNOPQRSTUVWXYZ

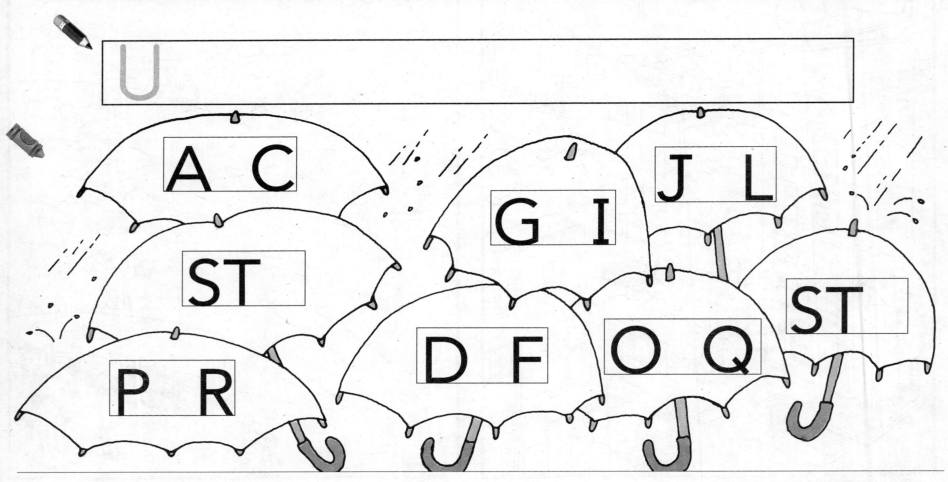

THEME 1: Look at Us!
Week Three
Letter Name *Uu*

Children
• write *U* in the box
• write the missing letters on the umbrellas

 Home Connection
I am learning about big *U*.
Let me show you all the big *U*'s
on the umbrellas. Then let's read
the sets of three letters on the
umbrellas.

58

Name _____

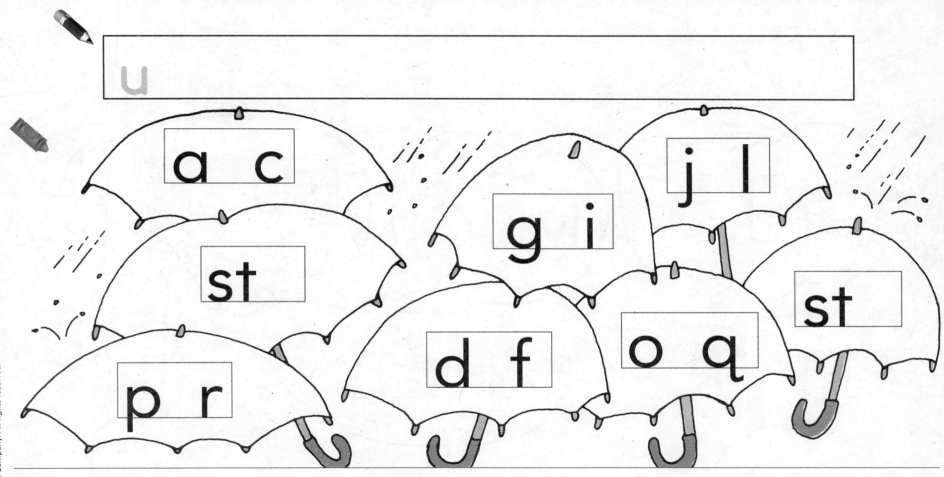

a b c d e f g h i j k l m n o p q r s t u v w x y z

u

a c

j l

g i

st

d f

o q

st

p r

THEME 1: Look at Us!
Week Three
Letter Name *Uu*

Children
- write *u* in the box
- write the missing letters on the umbrellas

 Home Connection
I am learning about small *u*.
Let me show you all the small *u*'s
on the umbrellas. Then let's read
the sets of three letters on the
umbrellas.

59

Name _____

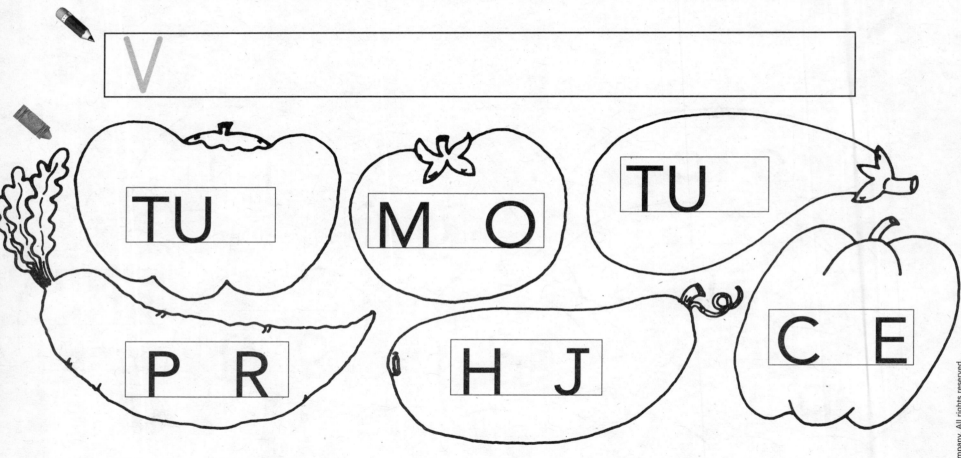

THEME 1: Look at Us!
Week Three
Letter Name *Vv*

Children
- write *V* in the box
- write the missing letters on the vegetables

Home Connection
I am learning about big *V*.
Let me show you all the big *V*'s
on the vegetables. Then let's
read the sets of three letters
on the vegetables.

Name _____

abcdefghijklmnopqrstuvwxyz

v

tu

m o

tu

p r

h j

c e

THEME 1: Look at Us!
Week Three
Letter Name *Vv*

Children
• write *v* in the box
• write the missing letters on the vegetables

 Home Connection
I am learning about small *v*.
Let me show you all the small *v*'s
on the vegetables. Then let's read
the sets of three letters on the
vegetables.

Name _____

1.

2.

Copyright © Houghton Mifflin Company. All rights reserved.

THEME 1: Look at Us!
Week Three *Here Are My Hands*
Noting Important Details

Children

1. draw lines from a body part to the object that goes with it

2. draw a picture of something they do with their hands, adding as much detail as they can

 Home Connection
Let me tell you about the picture I drew. Let's think of other things I can do with my hands.

62

Name _____

ABCDEFGHIJKLMNOPQRSTUVWXYZ

W

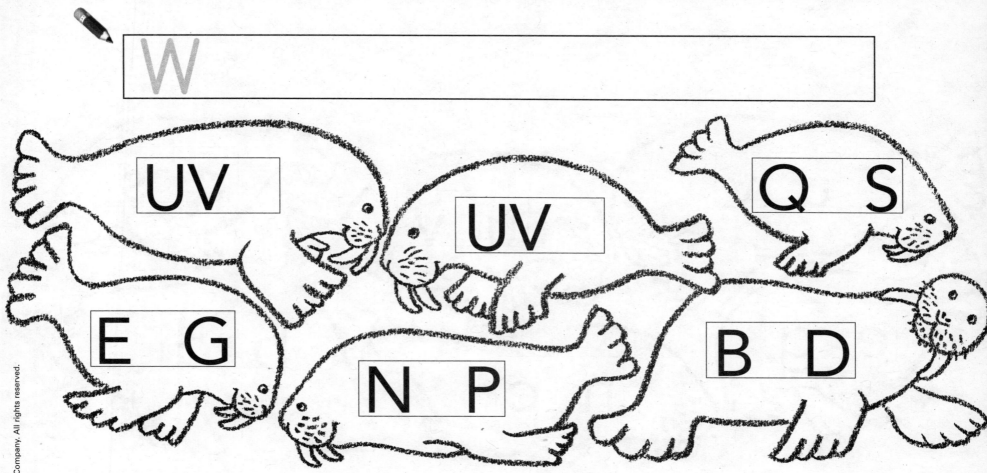

UV

UV

Q S

E G

N P

B D

THEME 1: Look at Us!
Week Three
Letter Name *Ww*

Children
• write *W* in the box
• write the missing letters on the walruses

 Home Connection
I am learning about big *W*.
Let me show you all the big *W*'s
on the walruses. Then let's read
the sets of three letters on the
walruses.

Name _____

a b c d e f g h i j k l m n o p q r s t u v w x y z

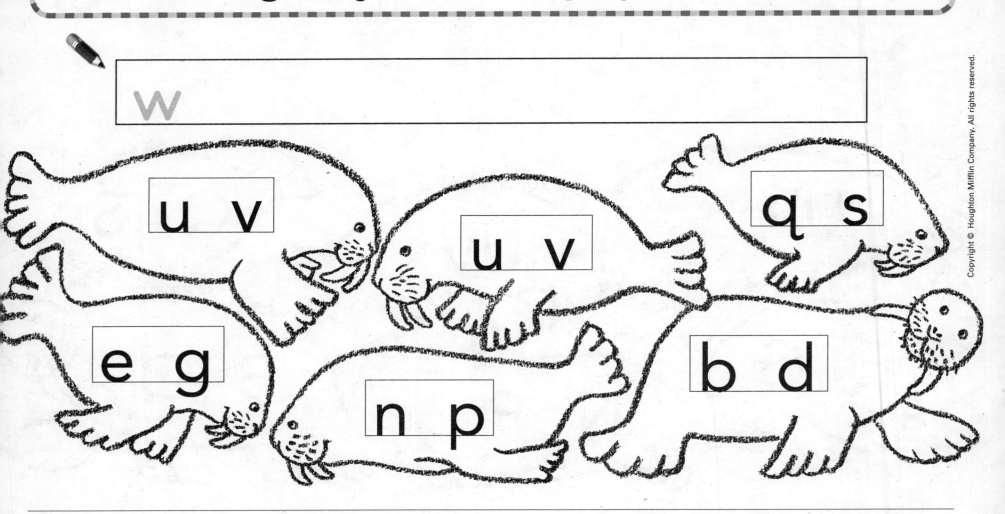

w

u v

u v

q s

e g

n p

b d

THEME 1: Look at Us!
Week Three
Letter Name *Ww*

64

Children
• write *w* in the box
• write the missing letters on the walruses

Home Connection
I am learning about small *w*.
Let me show you all the small *w*'s
on the walruses. Then let's read
the sets of three letters on the
walruses.

Name _____

ABCDEFGHIJKLMNOPQRSTUVWXYZ

X

V W

S U

A C

K M

V W

T V

THEME 1: Look at Us!
Week Three
Letter Name Xx

Children
- write *X* in the box
- write the missing letters on the x-rays

Home Connection
I am learning about big *X*.
Let me show you all the big *X*'s
on the x-rays. Then let's read
the sets of three letters
on the x-rays.

65

Name _____

a b c d e f g h i j k l m n o p q r s t u v w x y z

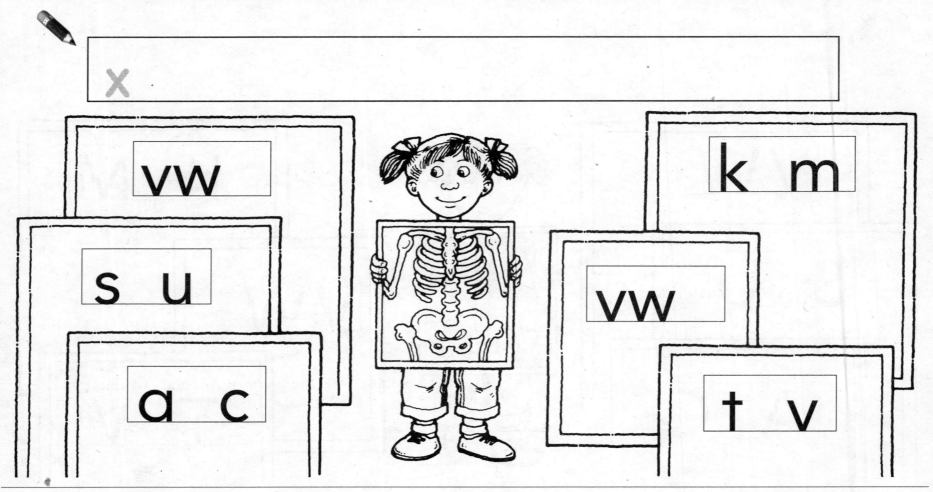

x

v w

s u

a c

k m

v w

t v

THEME 1: Look at Us!
Week Three
Letter Name *Xx*

Children
• write *x* in the box
• write the missing letters on the x-rays

 Home Connection
I am learning about small *x*.
Let me show you all the small *x*'s
on the x-rays. Then let's read the
sets of three letters on the x-rays.

66

Name _____

ABCDEFGHIJKLMNOPQRSTUVWXYZ

Y

WX   WX   K M

T V   P R   G I

THEME 1: Look at Us!
Week Three
Letter Name *Yy*

Children
• write *Y* in the box
• write the missing letters on the yaks

Home Connection
I am learning about big *Y*.
Let me show you all the big *Y*'s
on the yaks. Then let's read the
sets of three letters on the yaks.

Name _____

abcdefghijklmnopqrstuvwxyz

y

wx   wx   k m

t v   p r   g i

THEME 1: Look at Us!
Week Three
Letter Name *Yy*

Children
- write *y* in the box
- write the missing letters on the yaks

 Home Connection
I am learning about small *y*.
Let me show you all the small *y*'s
on the yaks. Then let's read the
sets of three letters on the yaks.

68

Name _____

ABCDEFGHIJKLMNOPQRSTUVWXYZ

Z

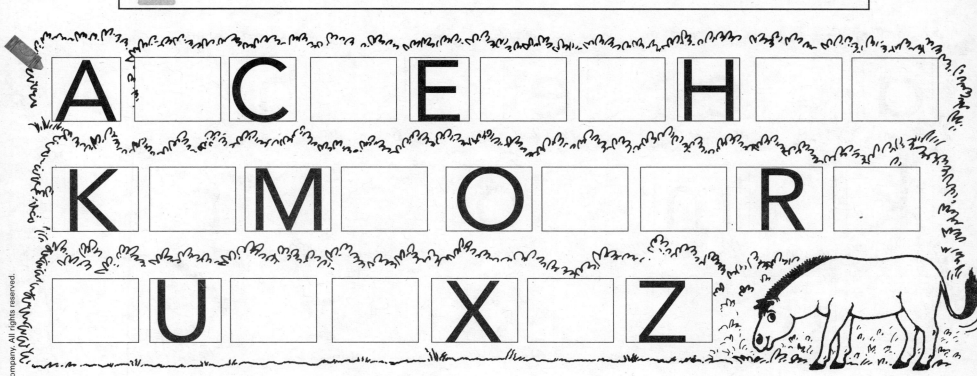

A C E H

K M O R

U X Z

THEME 1: Look at Us!
Week Three
Letter Name *Zz*

Children
- write *Z* in the box
- write the missing letters on the alphabet bushes
- make stripes on the zebra

 Home Connection
I am learning about big Z.
Let's read the whole alphabet
that ends with the zebra. Then
I'll show you the big Z
and the zebra.

69

Name _____

a b c d e f g h i j k l m n o p q r s t u v w x y z

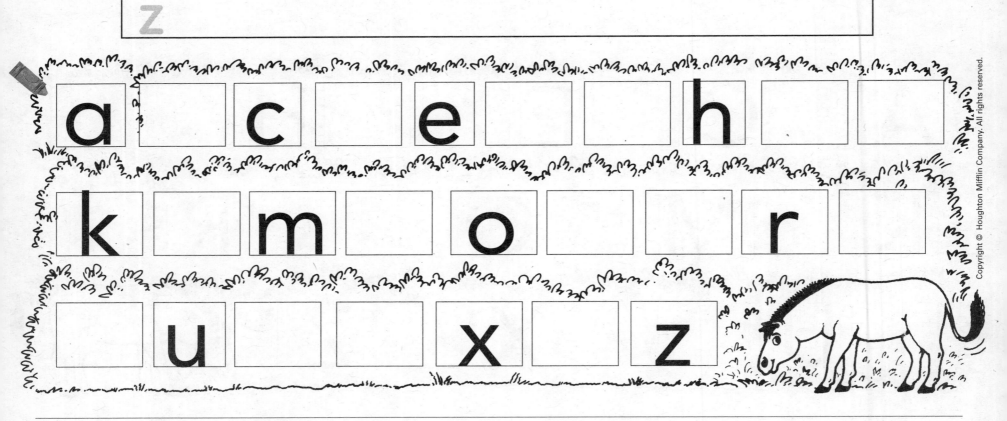

z

a c e [ ] h [ ]

k m o [ ] r [ ]

u [ ] x z

THEME 1: Look at Us!
Week Three
Letter Name *Zz*

Children
- write *z* in the box
- write the missing letters on the alphabet bushes
- make stripes on the zebra

Home Connection
I am learning about small *z*.
Let's read the whole alphabet
that ends with the zebra. Then
I'll show you the small *z* and
the zebra.

70

1 2 3

THEME 2: Colors All Around
Week One *I Need a Lunch Box*
Sequence of Events

Children
- think about what happened in the story
- write 1, 2, or 3 beside the pictures to show what happened first, next, and last
- color the pictures

 Home Connection
Let me tell you what happened in the story *I Need a Lunch Box*. We can point to the pictures as I tell each part.

71

Name _____

Monday

Tuesday

Wednesday

Thursday

Friday

THEME 2: Colors All Around
Week One *I Need a Lunch Box*
Responding

Children
- draw a different lunch box for each school day
- color each one a different color

Home Connection
Help me say the names of the days I go to school. Then I'll tell you about the lunch boxes I drew and the colors I used.

72

Name _____

I

1.

I _____

2.

_____

3.

_____

4.

I

THEME 2: Colors All Around
Week One
High-Frequency Word Review *I*

Children
for 1, 2, and 3,
• write the word *I* to complete the sentence
for 4,
• draw a picture to complete the sentence

 Home Connection
I am learning to read the word *I*.
Let me read the sentences to
you.

80   Just for fun, color the lunch boxes that show pictures of animals.

THEME 2: Colors All Around
Week Two *Caps of Many Colors*
Making Predictions

Children
- think about what the monkeys did in the story
- see the monkeys watching the children
- predict what the monkeys might do with a T-shirt, a camera, and a swing
- draw pictures of their predictions

Home Connection
Let me tell you a story called *Caps of Many Colors*. Then I'll tell you what the monkeys I drew are doing.

Name _____

THEME 2: Colors All Around
Week Two *Caps of Many Colors*
Responding

Children
• think about how the man in the story sold his caps
• make believe they have a shop that sells hats
• draw and color hats they might sell

 Home Connection
Let me tell you about the hats I might sell if I had a hat shop. Which hat is your favorite? Maybe we can draw more hats together.

Name _____

THEME 2: Colors All Around
Week Two
Phonemic Awareness: /m/

Children
- fix and color all the pictures on pages 83 and 84 whose names start like *Mimi Mouse*
- cut and paste pictures for that sound in the boxes on page 84
- draw something else whose name starts with that sound

 Home Connection
Let's name all the things on the front and back whose names start like *Mimi Mouse*.

Name _____

Name _____

1   2   3

THEME 2: Colors All Around
Week Three *How the Birds Got Their Colors*
Sequence of Events

Children
• draw lines from 1, 2, and 3 to what happened first, next, and last in the story
• color the pictures

 Home Connection
Let me tell you what happened first, next, and last in a story called *How the Birds Got Their Colors*. I'll point to the pictures as I tell it.

91

Name _____

THEME 2: Colors All Around
Week Three *How the Birds Got Their Colors*
Responding

Children
for 1 and 2,
• color the first picture and circle the picture beside it that shows what happens next
for 3,
• draw what happens first, next, and last in a story about how they would have rewarded the birds

Home Connection
Maybe we can find other make-believe stories at the library that tell why some things are the way they are.

Name _____

THEME 2: Colors All Around
Week Three
Phonemic Awareness: /r/

Children
- color all the pictures on pages 93 and 94 whose names start like *Reggie Rooster*
- cut and paste pictures for that sound in the boxes on page 94
- draw something else whose name starts with that sound

 Home Connection
Let's name all the things on the front and back whose names start like *Reggie Rooster*.

Name _____

THEME 2: Colors All Around
Week Three
Phonemic Awareness: /r/

Name _____

1.

2.

THEME 3: We're a Family
Week One *Jonathan and His Mommy*
Characters/Setting

Children
1. draw the family member the boy in the story took a walk with
2. color pictures of things the story characters saw when they jumped, skipped, and danced through their neighborhood together

Home Connection
Let me tell you about a story called *Jonathan and His Mommy* and what they saw when they took a walk.

99

Name _____

1.

2.

Copyright © Houghton Mifflin Company. All rights reserved.

THEME 3: We're a Family
Week One *Jonathan and His Mommy*
Responding

Children

1. draw themselves on a neighborhood walk with one of their family members

2. draw what they might see on their walk

 Home Connection
Let me tell you about the pictures I drew. On our next walk, let's see what we see that Jonathan and his mommy saw.

Name _____

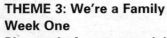

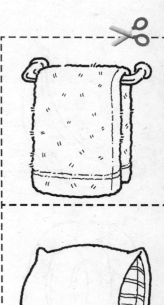

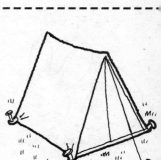

THEME 3: We're a Family
Week One
Phonemic Awareness: /t/

Children
- color all the pictures on pages 101 and 102 that start like *Tiggy Tiger*
- cut and paste the pictures for that sound in the boxes on page 101
- draw something else that starts with that sound

Home Connection
Let's name the things on the front and back that start like *Tiggy Tiger*.

Name _____

1.  **T t**

2.

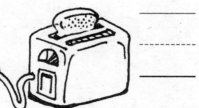

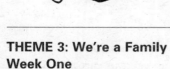

3.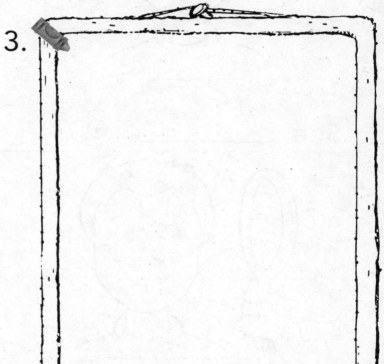

THEME 3: We're a Family
Week One
Phonics: Initial Consonant t

Children
• for 1 and 2, write *Tt* beside the pictures whose names start like *Tiggy Tiger*
• for 3, draw a picture with two things whose names start with the sound for *t*

 Home Connection
Today we learned the letter *t*. Let's look in an old newspaper for pictures whose names begin with the sound for *t*.

103

Name _____

1.

my

2.

See _____   **?**

I see _____  .

3.

4.

I see _____ 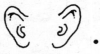 .

I see _____ .

THEME 3: We're a Family
Week One
High-Frequency Word *my*

Children
- read the sentences and write *my* to complete them
- draw the missing face parts to complete each picture

 Home Connection
Let me read this cartoon to you. Then we can cut it apart, make a cover and put it together into a comic book.

104

Name _____

THEME 3: We're a Family
Week One _Tortillas and Lullabies_
Characters/Setting, Responding

Children
- circle the pictures that show characters a story might be about
- color the pictures that show places a story might tell about
- draw a line between each character and a place it might be

 Home Connection
Let's think of some other characters who could be in stories and draw places they might be.

105

Name _____

T t   T   t

THEME 3: We're a Family
Week One
Phonics: Initial Consonant t

106

Children
- write *Tt* at the top
- name the pictures Tiggy Tiger thinks about
- color and write *t* beside pictures whose names begin with the sound for *t*

Home Connection
Next time we watch TV together, let's look for things whose names start with the sound for *t*.

Name _____

THEME 3: We're a Family
Week Two *Goldilocks and the Three Bears*
Drawing Conclusions

Children
- color the pictures that give clues about which of the Three Bears will be the most unhappy when the bears get home
- draw a picture of that bear

 Home Connection
Let me tell you about this picture. Which bear do you think will be most upset to see what Goldilocks has done?

109

Name _____

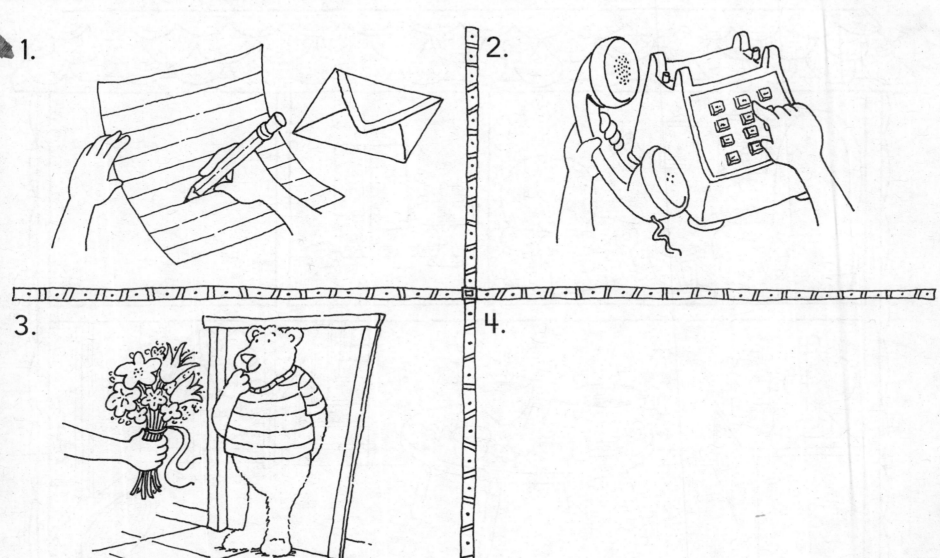

1.

2.

3.

4.

THEME 3: We're a Family
Week Two _Goldilocks and the Three Bears_
Responding

Children

- for 1, 2, and 3, color the picture that shows the way they might have told the bears they were sorry if they had been Goldilocks
- for 4, draw another way Goldilocks might have apologized

 Home Connection
Let me tell you about these pictures and how I think Goldilocks should have told the bears she was sorry.

Name _____

THEME 3: We're a Family
Week Two
Phonemic Awareness: /b/

Children
- color all the pictures on pages 111 and 112 that start like *Benny Bear*
- cut and paste the pictures for that sound in the boxes on page 112
- draw something else that starts with that sound

 Home Connection
Let's name all the things on the front and back that start like *Benny Bear*.

Name _____

Name _____

1.  **Bb** B b

2.  _____

 _____

 _____

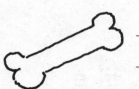 _____

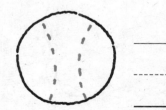 _____

3.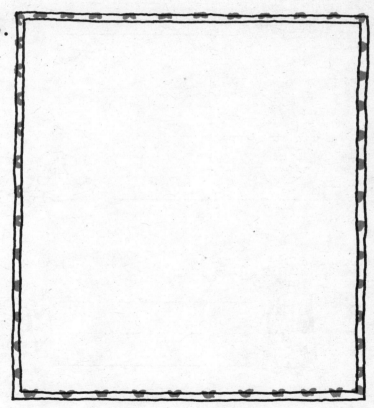

THEME 3: We're a Family
Week Two
Phonics: Initial Consonant b

Children
- for 1 and 2, write *Bb* beside pictures whose names start like *Benny Bear*
- for 3, draw a picture with two things whose names start with *b*

 Home Connection
Let me tell you which pictures start with the sound for *b*. Then let's look for other things that start with the sound for *b*.

113

Name _____

like

1.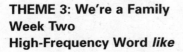

2.

I _____

3.

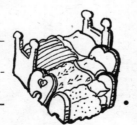

4.

I like

THEME 3: We're a Family
Week Two
High-Frequency Word *like*

Children
• for 1, 2, and 3, read the sentences and write *like* to complete them
• for 4, read the sentence and draw a picture to complete it

Home Connection
Let me read the sentences and pictures to you. Then I'll tell you about the picture I drew.

Name _____

1.

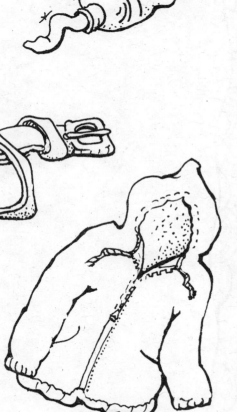

2.

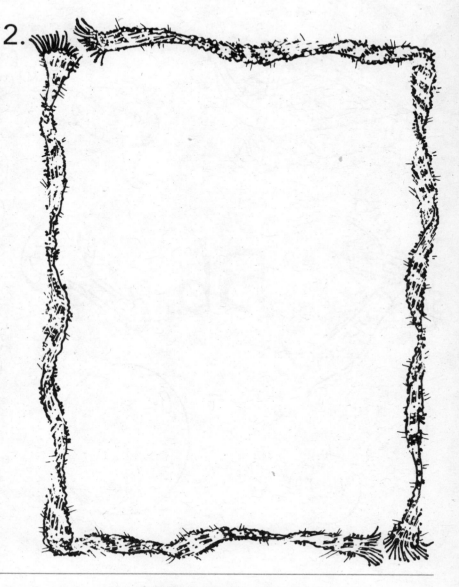

THEME 3: We're a Family
Week Two *Shoes from Grandpa*
Drawing Conclusions, Responding

Children
1. color what else Jessie's family members might get her if she gets the jeans she asked for at the end of the story
2. draw some kind of clothing they might wish for as a birthday gift

 Home Connection
Let me tell you a story called
Shoes from Grandpa. Then let's
talk about who the members of
our family are.

115

Name _____

1.

2.

b Bb   B _____ b

THEME 3: We're a Family
Week Two
Phonics: Initial Consonant _b_

Children
- draw lines from pictures whose names start with the sound for _b_ to _Bb_
- draw something else for that sound in the box with Benny Bear

Home Connection
Let me tell you about the picture I drew. Then let's look for more things whose names start with the sound for _b_.

Name _____

THEME 3: We're a Family
Week Three *The Amazing Little Porridge Pot*
Comprehension, Drawing Conclusions

Children
- draw beside each picture what they think the woman must do to solve the problem she finds in that room

 Home Connection
Let me tell you about what the woman found when she came home and about the pictures I drew.

119

Name _____

THEME 3: We're a Family
Week Three _The Amazing Little Porridge Pot_
Responding

Children
- look at the pictures that show different endings for the story
- color the picture that shows the ending they might have chosen to write for the story

 Home Connection
If I had written the story, _The Amazing Little Porridge Pot_, I might have written a different ending for it. Let me tell you about it.

120

Name _____

THEME 3: We're a Family
Week Three
Phonemic Awareness: /n/

Children
• color all the pictures on pages 121 and 122 that start like *Nyle Noodle*
• cut and paste pictures for that sound in the boxes on page 122
• draw something else that starts with that sound

Home Connection
Let's name all the things on the front and back that start like *Nyle Noodle.*

Name _____

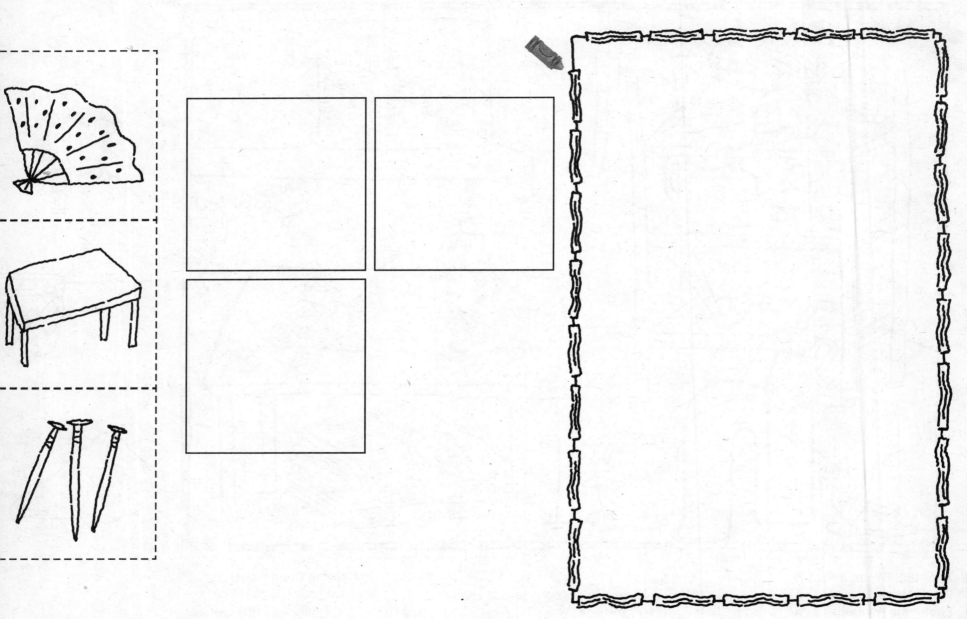

THEME 3: We're a Family
Week Three
Phonemic Awareness: /n/

Name _____

1.

2.

THEME 3: We're a Family
Week Three *Tortillas and Lullabies*
Character/Setting, Responding

Children

1. think about something one of the people in the story did in the kitchen and draw a picture of her doing that

2. think about something one of the people in the story did in the garden and draw a picture of her doing that

 Home Connection
Let me tell you the story we heard today called *Tortillas and Lullabies.* Then maybe we can look at pictures of my grandmothers and great-grandmothers.

123

Name _____

N n N n

Children
- write *Nn* at the top
- name the pictures Nyle Noodle thinks about
- color and write *n* beside pictures whose names begin with the sound for *n*

Home Connection
Let's look in a newspaper for pictures of things that start like *Nyle Noodle*.

Name _____

1.

2.

3.

THEME 4: Friends Together
Week One *Friends at School*
Organization and Summarizing

Children
1. think about the friends in the story and color the pictures
2. draw something one group of friends did together in the story
3. color those things the friends played with in the story

 Home Connection
Today my teacher read us a story *Friends at School*. Let me tell it to you. I'll use the pictures to help me remember parts of it.

129

Name _____

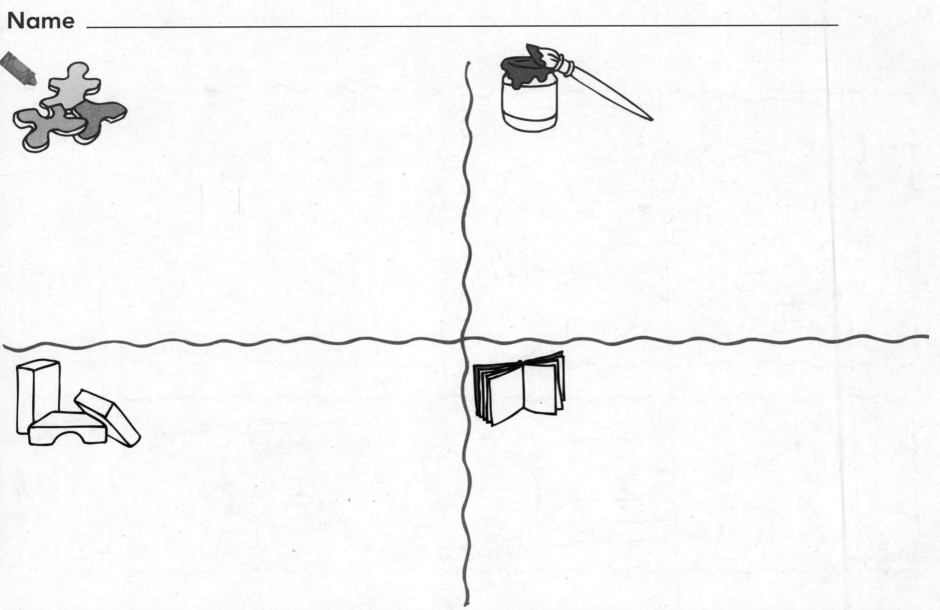

THEME 4: Friends Together
Week One _Friends at School_
Responding

Children
• draw what they and a friend might do with each of the school-related things

 Home Connection
Ask me what kinds of things I like to do with my friends. What did you like to do with your friends at school when you were my age?

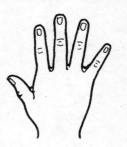

THEME 4: Friends Together
Week One
Phonemic Awareness: /h/

Children
- color all the pictures on pages 131 and 132 that start like *Hattie Horse*
- cut and paste pictures for that sound in the boxes on page 132
- draw something else that starts with that sound

 Home Connection
Let's name all the things on the front and the back that start like *Hattie Horse*.

131

Name _____

Name _____

 1. 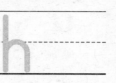 H h H ___ ___ h ___ ___  ___ ___  ___ ___

2.

 _____

 _____

 _____

 _____

 _____

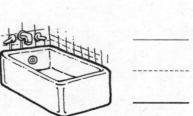 _____

3.

THEME 4: Friends Together
Week One
Phonics: Initial Consonant _h_

Children
- for 1 and 2, write _h_ beside the pictures whose names start like _Hattie Horse_
- for 3, draw a picture of two things whose names start with _h_

 Home Connection
Today we learned the letter _h_. Help me find pictures in books of things that start like _Hattie Horse._

133

Name _____

a

1.

See _ _ _ _ _ _ _ _ _ .

😊 ☹️

2.

See _ _ _ _ _ _ _ _ _ .

😊 ☹️

3.

See _ _ _ _ _ _ _ _ _ .

😊 ☹️

4.

See _____

·

THEME 4: Friends Together
Week One
High-Frequency Word: *a*

Children
For 1, 2, and 3
• read the sentences and write *a* to complete them
• mark yes (smile) or no (frown) to show whether the pictures go with the sentences
For 4, read the sentence and draw something they would like to see

 Home Connection
Let me read these questions to you and we can see if you answer them the same way I did.

Name _____

A B C D E

F G H I J K

L M N O P

Q R S T U

V W X Y Z

My name is

_____

- -

_____

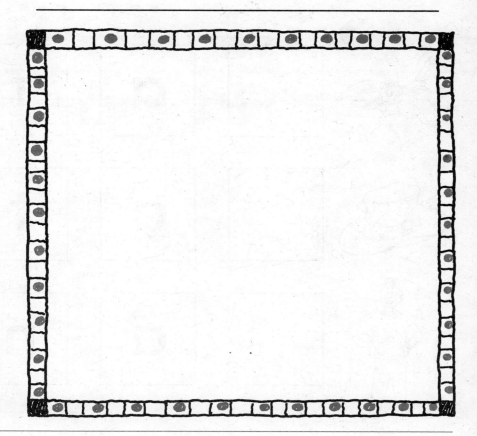

THEME 4: Friends Together
Week One *Aaron and Gayla's Alphabet Book*
Text Organization & Summarizing, Responding

Children
- name the letters of the alphabet
- color the letter that begins their own name
- write their name on the line
- draw a picture of themselves

Home Connection
Will you sing the ABC song
with me? We can point to the
letters as we sing.

135

Name _____

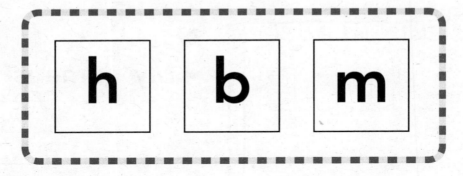

h	b	m

 | | a | t | | I see a _____ .

 | | a | t | | I see a _____ .

 | | a | n | | I see a _____ .

THEME 4: Friends Together
Week One
Phonics: *h,* **Short** *a* **Words**

Children
- write letters to complete the picture names (*bat, hat, man*)
- write each word to complete the sentences

Home Connection
Let's cut out the letter squares, mix them up, and build the words *hat, bat,* and *man* again.

Name _____

s	**a**	**t**
r	**a**	**n**
b	**a**	**t**

_____

- - - - - - - - - - - - - - - - - - -

_____

- - - - - - - - - - - - - - - - - - -

_____

- - - - - - - - - - - - - - - - - - -

_____

- - - - - - - - - - - - - - - - -

A cat _____ .

_____

- - - - - - - - - - - - - - - - -

A fat rat _____ .

_____

- - - - - - - - - - - - - - - - -

I see Nat at _____ .

THEME 4: Friends Together
Week One
Phonics: Short _a_ Words

Children
- add letters to build *sat*, *ran*, and *bat*
- write each word to complete the sentences

Home Connection
Would you like to listen to me
read the words and sentences on
this page? Then we can make up
some other short *a* words.

137

Name _____

| a | see | like |

1. _____

I see ___ c A H ___ cat I like.

2. _____

I see a hat I _____.

3. _____

I ___ a bat I like.

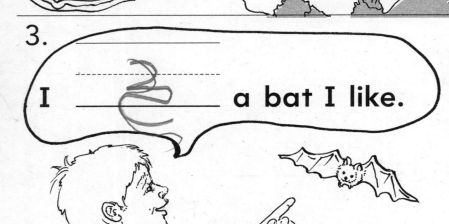

4.

I see a

Children
• for 1, 2, and 3 write *a*, *see*, or *like* to complete the sentences
• for 4, draw a picture to complete the sentence

Home Connection
Let me read these cartoons to you. Then we can cut them into four smaller pages and make a comic book and a cover for it.

Name AVery

1.

2.

THEME 4: Friends Together
Week Two *The Lion and the Mouse*
Cause and Effect

Children
1. color what made the mouse afraid
2. color the picture that shows what its promise to the lion caused the mouse to do

 Home Connection
Let me tell you the story *The Lion and the Mouse*. Then you'll know what caused the mouse to chew a hole in the net.

139

Name _____

1.

2.

THEME 4: Friends Together
Week Two *The Lion and the Mouse*
Responding

140

Children

1. imagine they were the author of the story and draw a picture to show a different way the mouse might help the lion

2. draw a picture of a friend in need of help and how they might help that friend

 Home Connection
Today we heard a story called *The Lion and the Mouse*. Will you listen as I tell it to you? Then I'll tell you about the pictures I drew.

Name _____

THEME 4: Friends Together
Week Two
Phonemic Awareness: /v/

Children
- color all the pictures on pages 141 and 142 that start like *Vinny Volcano*
- cut and paste pictures for that sound in the boxes on page 142
- draw something else that starts with that sound

Home Connection
I'll name the pictures on the front and back that start like *Vinny Volcano*. Then let's find things around the house that start with that sound.

141

Name _____

1.

2. V v

V V v

Vv

THEME 4: Friends Together
Week Two
Phonics: Initial Consonant _v_

Children

1. draw lines from pictures whose names begin
   with the sound for _v_ to the letters _Vv_

2. write _Vv_ at the top and complete the picture
   of the exploding volcano

 Home Connection
Today I finished this exploding
volcano picture. Let me show it
to you. Then I can tell you
about the other pictures that
begin with the sound for _v_.

Name _____

cat

to _____

bat

_____
I like _____ see my cat.

_____
I like _____ see a bat.

THEME 4: Friends Together
Week Two
High-Frequency Word: *to*

Children
- read the words that name the pictures and write *to*
- read the sentences and write *to* to complete them
- draw pictures to go with the sentences

 Home Connection
I can read these sentences to you. Then I'll tell you about the pictures I drew to go with the sentences.

144

Name _____

1.

2.

THEME 4: Friends Together
Week Two *My Dad and I*
Cause and Effect

Children

1. circle the pictures that show something the father and son in the story played together, because they are friends

2. draw a picture of something they themselves play with someone, because they are friends

Home Connection
We heard a story called *My Dad and I* today. Let me tell it to you. Then I'll tell you about the picture I drew and why I drew it.

145

Name _____

vat   hat   van

See my _____ .

See my _____ .

See my _____ .

THEME 4: Friends Together
Week Two
Phonics: _v_, Short _a_ Words

Children
• read the sentences and write the short _a_ words to complete them
• mark the smile (yes) or the frown (no) to show whether the pictures go with the sentences

Home Connection
Let me read the questions to you and tell you about my answers. Then will you help me make up more sentences with those words?

146

Name _____

s	m	v

	a	t	I like my _____ .
	a	n	See my _____ .
	a	t	A cat _____ .

THEME 4: Friends Together
Week Two
Phonics: Short _a_ Words

Children
• write letters to complete the picture names (_mat, van, sat_)
• write each word to complete the sentences

 Home Connection
Let me read the sentences to you. Then we can cut out the letter squares, mix them up, and build the words _mat, van,_ and _sat._

147

to   a   My   like

I like _____ bat a .

_____ cat sat!

I see _____ fat bat.

I _____ my hat.

THEME 4: Friends Together
Week Two
High-Frequency Words Review: to, a, my, like

Children
- read the cartoons
- write a, to, my, and like to complete the sentences
- complete the last picture

Home Connection
Today I finished this cartoon. Let me read it to you. Then we can cut apart the four cartoon boxes, make a book with them, and read it to someone else.

148

Name _____

THEME 4: Friends Together
Week Three *Stone Soup*
Cause and Effect

Children
- think about the story *Stone Soup* and how the man tricked the villagers into making wonderful soup
- color those ingredients that caused the soup to become so tasty and add two more things that could be added to make it even better

 Home Connection
We heard the story *Stone Soup* today. Ask me to tell you about it. I can point to the pictures I colored as I tell that part of the story.

149

Name _____

THEME 4: Friends Together
Week Three *Stone Soup*
Responding

Children
- think about whether the stone had anything to do with making the soup tasty
- imagine how the story would be different if the man asked for help making some stone pizza instead
- draw their ideas

 Home Connection
Let me tell you about my picture and the story I drew it for.

Name _____

THEME 4: Friends Together
Week Three
Phonemic Awareness: /c/

Children
- color all the pictures on pages 151 and 152 that start like *Callie Cat*
- cut and paste pictures for that sound in the boxes on page 152
- draw something else that starts with that sound

 Home Connection
Let's name all the things on the front and back that start like *Callie Cat.*

151

Name _____

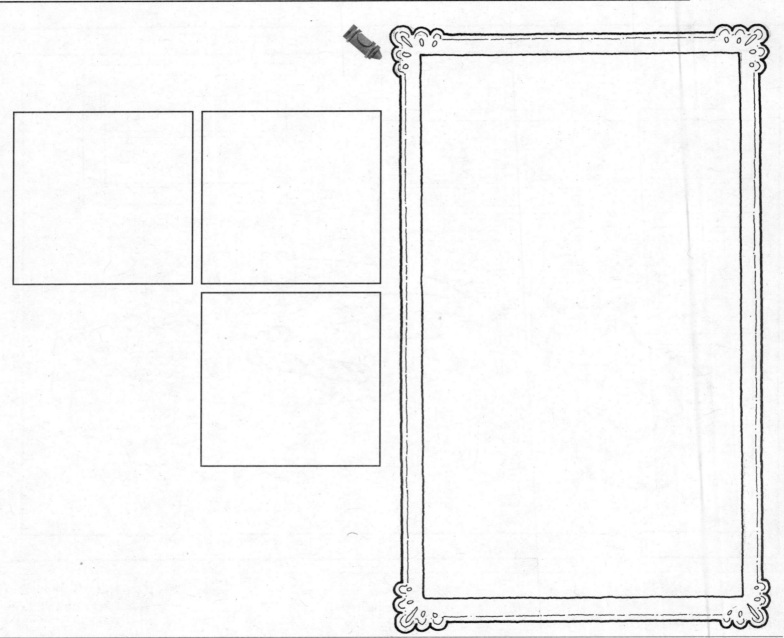

A B C D E F _ _ _
H I J K L M N
O P Q R S T
U V W X Y Z

A B _ D E F G
H I J K L M N
O P Q R S T
U V W X Y Z

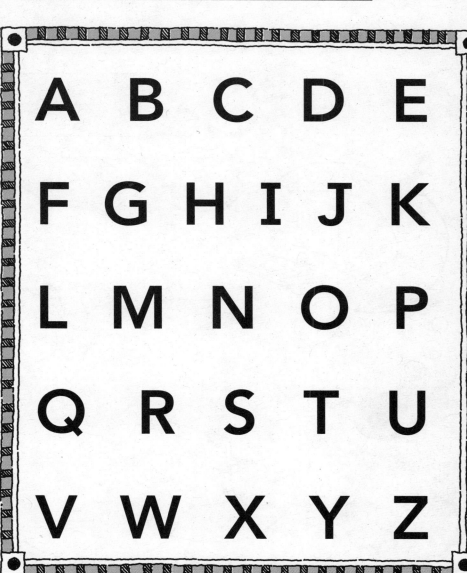

A B C D E
F G H I J K
L M N O P
Q R S T U
V W X Y Z

THEME 4: Friends Together
Week Three *Aaron and Gayla's*
Alphabet Book
Text Organization and Summarizing,
Responding

Children
- write the letters missing from the alphabet
- play this game in pairs: one partner covers a letter with a coin or token, and the other tells what letter is covered

 Home Connection
Today I learned to play "Hide the Letter." I can teach it to you.

153

C c   C _____   c _____

THEME 4: Friends Together
Week Three
Phonics: Initial Consonant c

Children
- write *C c* at the top
- name the pictures *Callie Cat* thinks about
- color and write *c* beside pictures whose names begin with the sound for *c*

Home Connection
Today we learned the letter *c*. Can you help me find a few things around our house that start like *Callie Cat*?

Name _____

a   to   see

1. _____

I sat _____ see a 🐕.

2. _____

I sat to _____ a 🦢.

3. _____

I sat to see _____ 🐍.

4. I sat to see a cat.

THEME 4: Friends Together
Week Three
High-Frequency Words Review: *a, to*

Children
- for 1, 2, and 3, read the cartoons, write *a, to,* and *see* to complete the sentences, and color the cartoons
- for 4, draw a cartoon to go with the sentence

 Home Connection
Listen while I read these cartoons to you. Then we can cut them apart to make a comic book.

155

cat   man   fat   sat

See my fat _____ .

I see a _____ .

My _____ cat _____ .

THEME 4: Friends Together
Week Three
Phonics: c, Short a Words

Children
- write short *a* words to complete the sentences
- mark smile (yes) or frown (no) to show whether the picture goes with the sentence

Home Connection
Let's write *cat*, *man*, *fat*, and *sat* and make up some more sentences using these words.

156

Name _____

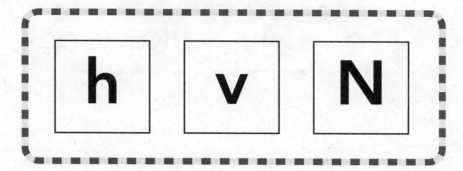

  | a | t

I see _____ at bat.

 | a | n

My _____ is tan.

 | a | t

I like my _____.

THEME 4: Friends Together
Week Three
Phonics: Short *a* Words

Children
• write *h*, *v*, or *N* to complete the words (*Nat*, *van*, *hat*)
• write each word to complete the sentences about the pictures

 Home Connection
Can I read these sentences to you? Then we can cut out the letter squares, mix them up, and use them to build the words *Nat*, *van*, and *hat* again.

Name _____

to My like a

1. _____

    _ _ _ _ _ _ _ _ _ _ _ _ _ _

_____ cat sat.

    _ _ _ _ _ _ _ _ _ _

    _ _ _ _ _ _ _ _ _ _ _ _

I _____ my cat.

2. _____

    _ _ _ _ _ _ _ _ _ _ _ _

See _____ rat?

3. _____

    _ _ _ _ _ _ _ _ _ _ _ _

My cat ran _____ see a
rat.

4.

THEME 4: Friends Together
Week Three
High-Frequency Words Review: *a, to, my, like*

Children
- for 1, 2, and 3, read the sentences and write words to complete them
- for 4, draw a picture to show how the story might end

Home Connection
I can read these sentences to you. Then I'll tell you about the picture I made that shows how the story ends.

158

Name _____

1.

2.

THEME 5: Let's Count!
Week One: *Benny's Pennies*
Categorize & Classify

Children
1. draw presents Benny bought for his family
2. draw presents Benny bought for his family's pets

 Home Connection
Ask me to tell you about a story
called *Benny's Pennies*.

159

Name _____

1.

2.

THEME 5: Let's Count!
Week One *Benny's Pennies*
Responding

Children
1. draw things they would buy members of their own families and the pennies it might take to buy each
2. draw things they would buy for a friend and the pennies it might take to buy each

 Home Connection
Can you help me think of some good gifts for our family?

Name _____

THEME 5: Let's Count!
Week One
Phonemic Awareness: /p/

Children
- color all the pictures on pages 161–162 that start like *Pippa Pig*
- cut and paste pictures for that sound in the boxes on page 162, then draw something else that starts with that sound

 Home Connection
Let's name all the things on the front and the back that start like *Pippa Pig*.

161

Name _____

THEME 5: Let's Count!
Week One
Phonemic Awareness: /p/

162

Name _____

1.  **P** **Pp** P _____ p _____ 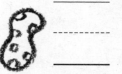 _____  _____

2.

3.

THEME 5: Let's Count!
Week One
Phonics: Initial Consonant _p_

Children
• for 1 and 2, color and write _p_ beside the pictures whose names start like _Pippa Pig_
• for 3, draw pictures of two _p_ things

 Home Connection
Today we learned the letter _p_.
Help me find pictures of things that start with the sound for _p_.

163

Name _____

and

1. _____

See my _____ cat?

2. _____

See my _____ cat?

3. _____

See my _____ cat?

4. _____

See my _____ cat.

THEME 5: Let's Count!
Week One
High-Frequency Word *and*

Children
• read the sentences and write *and* to complete them
• mark smile (yes) or frown (no) to answer the questions
• draw the last picture

 Home Connection
Let me read these sentences to you.

164

Name _____

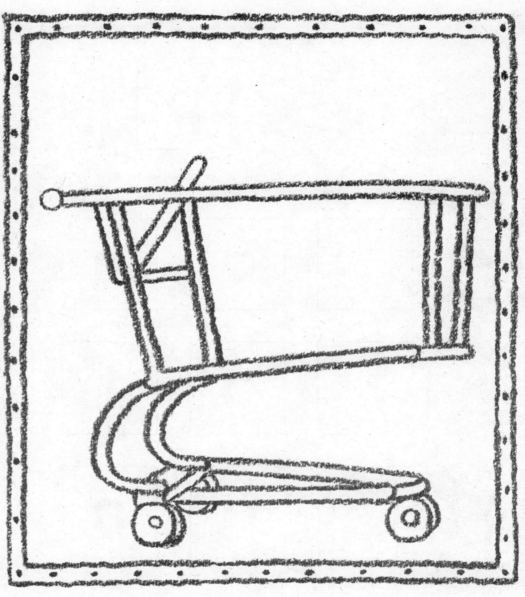

THEME 5: Let's Count!
Week One *Feast for 10*
Categorize and Classify, Responding

Children
- color things they saw in the story *Feast for 10*
- draw foods in the cart they would buy for their own family's meal

 Home Connection
Today we heard a story called *Feast for 10*. Ask me to tell you about it.

Name _____

p	r	v

  | a | n |

I see a bat _____.

  | a | t |

I see a _____ mat.

 | a | n |

I see a cat _____.

 THEME 5: Let's Count!
Week One
Phonics: *p*, Short *a* Words

166

Children
- write letters to complete the picture names (*pan*, *rat*, or *van*)
- write each word to complete the sentences

 Home Connection
I can read these sentences. We can cut out the letter squares and build the words again. Then, we can make up some other silly hats.

Name _____

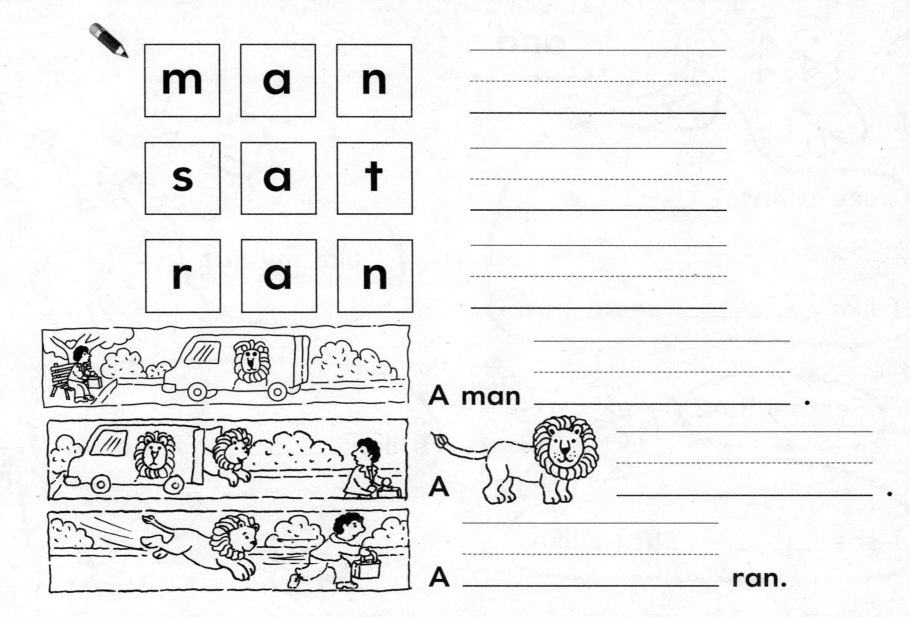

m	a	n
s	a	t
r	a	n

_____

_____

_____

_____

A man _____ .

A _____ .

A _____ ran.

THEME 5: Let's Count!
Week One
Phonics: Short *a* Words

Children
- add letters to short *a* to build the words *man*, *sat*, *ran*
- write these words to complete the sentences

 Home Connection
Please listen to me read these words and sentences.

Name _____

and   to   a

1. I see a hat, _____
   _____

   I like _____ see a hat.

2. I like my hat.

3. See my hat?

   I see _____ hat I like.

4. I like _____ see a hat.

Children
• read the sentences in the cartoon and write
  and, _to_, or _a_ to complete them

Home Connection
I'll read this cartoon to you. Then
we can cut it apart to make a
comic book.

Name _____

THEME 5: Let's Count!
Week Two *Counting Noodles*
Beginning/Middle/End

Children

1. think about the beginning of the story
2. finish the picture to show the middle of it
3. draw what the Noodles kept on doing at the end of the story

Home Connection
Let me tell you the story, *Counting Noodles*. Then we can count the Noodle family.

169

Name _____

THEME 5: Let's Count!
Week Two *Counting Noodles*
Responding

Children
• think about a new story they might tell about the Noodles on a farm
• draw their ideas for their new story

Home Connection
This is a picture for a story about the Noodles on a farm. Let me tell you about it.

Name _____

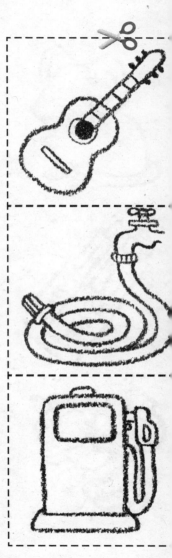

THEME 5: Let's Count!
Week Two
Phonemic Awareness: /g/

Children
- color all the pictures on pages 171 and 172 that start like *Gertie Goose*
- cut and paste the pictures for that sound in the boxes on page 172, then draw something else that starts with that sound

 Home Connection
Let's name all the things on the front and the back that start like *Gertie Goose.*

171

Name _____

Name _____

1.

2.

Gg

THEME 5: Let's Count!
Week Two
Phonics: Initial Consonant *g*

Children
1. draw lines from pictures whose names start
   with the sound for *g* to the letters *Gg*
2. write *Gg* on the lines and draw something else
   that starts with the sound for *g*.

 Home Connection
Today we learned the letter *g*.
Help me find magazine pictures
whose names start with the
sound for *g*.

Name _____

van

go

bat

A van can _____ to a .

A bat can _____ to a .

THEME 5: Let's Count!
Week Two
High-Frequency Word *go*

Children

• read the sentences and write *go* to complete them

• complete the pictures for each sentence

 Home Connection

I can read these sentences to you. Let's write *go, van,* and *bat,* then we can make up other sentences using these words.

174

Name _____

THEME 5: Let's Count!
Week Two *Ten Little Puppies*
Beginning/Middle/End, Responding

Children

1. count the puppies and draw more to show how many the boy had at the beginning

2. draw what one of the puppies did in the middle of the story

 Home Connection
Let me tell you the story *Ten Little Puppies*. Then I'll tell you about the pictures.

175

Name _____

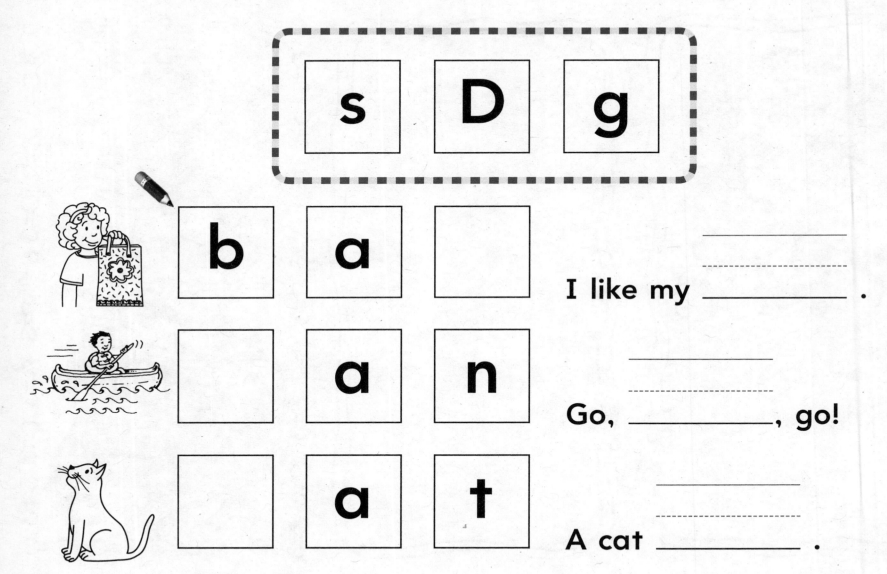

| s | D | g |

I like my _____.

Go, _____, go!

A cat _____.

THEME 5: Let's Count!
Week Two
Phonics: *g*, Short *a* Words

Children
• write letters to complete the picture names *bag*, *Dan*, and *sat*
• write each word to finish the sentences

Home Connection
Let's cut out the letter squares, I'll read the sentences, then we can build *bag*, *Dan*, and *sat* again.

Name _____

$$\boxed{\textbf{man} \quad \textbf{can} \quad \textbf{ran}}$$

_____

I _____ go.

My cat _____ .

A _____ ran.

THEME 5: Let's Count!
Week Two
Phonics: -an Words

Children
- read the sentences and write words ending in -an to complete them (*can, ran, man*)
- mark the smile (yes) or the frown (no) to show whether the pictures go with the sentences

 Home Connection
I'll read these sentences. Then we can write *can, ran* and *man* on a paper and make up more sentences using them.

177

Name _____

my and go

1.

Can I go _____ see?

2.

See _____ van go?

3.

Can I _____ and see?

4.

I see the hat.

Children
- read the cartoon and write *my*, *and*, *go* to complete what the children are saying
- complete the picture for 4 so it goes with the sentence

Home Connection
Today I finished this cartoon. We could cut these four cartoon boxes apart and make them into a comic book.

Name _____

1.

2.

3.

THEME 5: Let's Count!
Week Three *Peace and Quiet*
Beginning/Middle/End

Children

1. think about what happened in the beginning

2. color the picture that shows what happened in the middle

3. draw what the man and woman did at the end

 Home Connection
Let me tell you the story *Peace and Quiet*. I'll use the pictures to help me remember what happened at the beginning, in the middle, and at the end.

179

Name _____

1.

2.

THEME 5: Let's Count!
Week Three _Peace and Quiet_
Responding

Children
1. circle the things that are making noises
2. draw a picture of what they might do to make the noisy things quiet

 Home Connection
Let's take a walk around our house and find some things that make noises that might keep us awake.

180

Name _____

Name _____

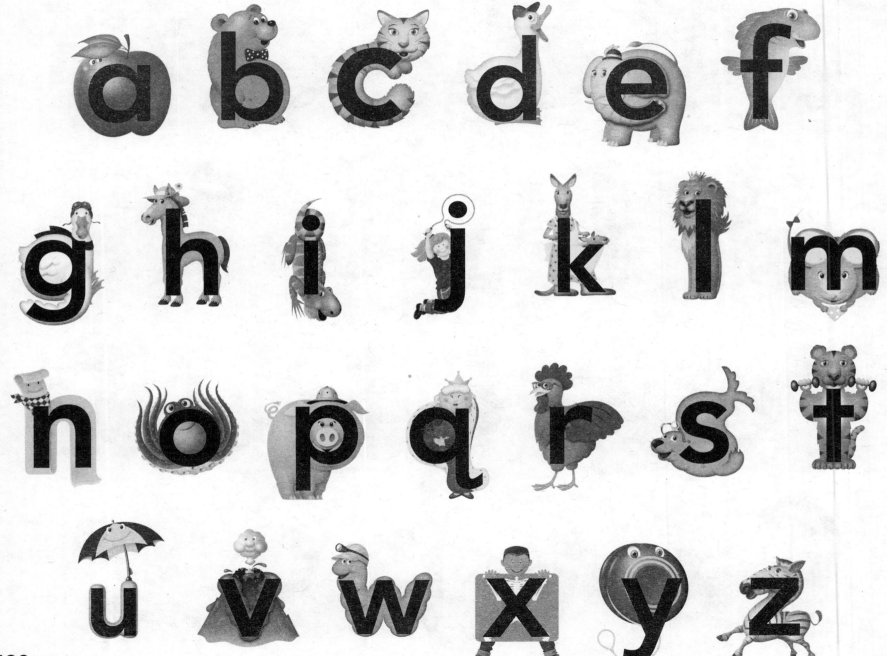

Word and Picture Book

Contents

 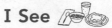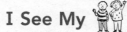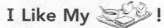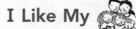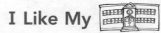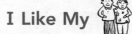

I see my .

I see my .

High-frequency word: *my*

I See My

I see my  .

I see my .

Theme 3, Week 1, Day 2

I see my  .

I see my .

I see my  .

I see my .

High-frequency word: *my*

Theme 3, Week 1, Day 2

I See My

I see my 🖌️ .

I see my .

I see my 👨 .

I see my 🐕 .

High-frequency words: *I, see, my*

Theme 3, Week 1, Day 5

I see my .

I see my .

I see my .

I see my .

High-frequency words: *I, see, my*

Theme 3, Week 1, Day 5

I Like My  !

I like my .

I like  .

I like my .

I like my  !

High-frequency word: *like*

I like my  .

I like  .

I like my  .

I like  .

2

High-frequency word: *like*

Theme 3, Week 2, Day 2

3

I Like My

I see my .

I like my .

I see my .

I like my !

High-frequency words: *I, see, like, my*

I see my .

I like my .

I see my .

I like my .

High-frequency words: *I, see, like, my*

Theme 3, Week 2, Day 5

I Like My

I see my **.**

I like my **.**

I see my 🍎🥛 .

I like my 🍎🥛 .

2

4

High-frequency words: *I, see, like, my*

Theme 3, Week 3, Day 2

I see my .

I like my .

I see my 🚪.

I like my 🚪.

High-frequency words: *I, see, like, my*

I Like

I see my .

I like my .

I see my .

I like my .

High-frequency words: *I, see, like, my*

I see my  .

I like my 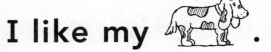 .

I see my 🐱 .

I like my 🐱 .

High-frequency words: *I, see, like, my*

Theme 3, Week 3, Day 5

I See a

I see a  .

I see a  .

I see a . (slide)

I see a . (swing set)

4

High-frequency word: *a*

Theme 4, Week 1, Day 2

1

I see a  .

I see a .

I see a .

I see a .

High-frequency word: *a*

Theme 4, Week 1, Day 2

I Like

I see a 🌈 .

I like 🌈🌈 .

I see a ☁ .

I see 🌧 .

High-frequency words: *I, see, my, like, a*

Theme 4, Week 1, Day 5

I see my .

I see my .

I see a .

I like .

2

I Like

I like to .

I like .

I like to .

I like to  .

High-frequency word: *to*

Theme 4, Week 2, Day 2

I like to  .

I like to  .

I like to  .

I like to  .

High-frequency word: *to*

Theme 4, Week 2, Day 2

I Like My

 I see my  .

I like my  .

I like to  .

I  to  .

High-frequency words: *I, see, like, my, a, to*

I see my  .

I to my .

I see a .

I see a .

High-frequency words: *I, see, like, my, a, to*

Theme 4, Week 2, Day 5

I Like My

I like my .

I like to see my .

I like my .

I like to my .

4

High-frequency words: *I, see, like, my, a, to*

1

I see a .

I see a .

I see a .

I like my .

High-frequency words: *I, see, like, my, a, to*

Theme 4, Week 3, Day 2

I Like to

I see a 📖.

I like to  📖.

I like to 📖.

I like to 📖 to my 👧👧.

High-frequency words: *I, see, like, my, a, to*

My 🧒🧒 **like to** 🏃‍♀️ .

My 🧒🧒 **like to** 😄 .

My 🧒🧒 **like my** 📖 .

My 🧒🧒 **like to** 🙆 .

2

High-frequency words: *I, see, like, my, a, to*

3